Managing Repair & Restoration Projects:

A Congregation's How-to Guide

The New York Landmarks Conservancy is proud to introduce *Managing Repair & Restoration Projects: A Congregation's How-to Guide.* It is the product of years of in-the-field experience, a collection of advice that has long been given informally, but never before collected in one comprehensive publication.

Managing Repair & Restoration Projects takes readers through the steps of planning and administering repair and restoration projects for older houses of worship. It is not a technical manual, nor a guide to construction lingo. This is a how-to-be-in-charge text. It aims to lead laypeople and clergy through the process of identifying and executing a project in a way that makes sense for both the building and its users.

The Landmarks Conservancy urges readers to use and share this book. It has been written in a simple, clear style and designed for readability and easy photocopying or scanning (subject to the copyright notice at left). The following pages of introduction describe the book's format, which includes scenarios, a glossary, and a comprehensive appendix to illustrate the concepts presented.

The New York Landmarks Conservancy's Sacred Sites Program is dedicated to helping congregations across the State repair their historic houses of worship. To this end, the Conservancy provides them with grants and technical assistance, coordinates how-to workshops, and publishes *Common Bond,* an educational journal addressing the administrative and technical aspects of building maintenance. The Conservancy has also published *Inspecting and Maintaining Religious Properties,* an instructive manual, and now adds *Managing Repair & Restoration Projects* to its collection.

For more information about the Landmarks Conservancy or the Sacred Sites Program, visit www.nylandmarks.org or call 800-880-NYLC.

▶ Please note

This book is a general text intended to introduce laypeople to the process of managing a repair project. It does not aim to give professional advice on legal, architectural, contracting, insurance, or preservation matters. Readers are encouraged to pursue subjects of interest or pertinence using the Resource section in the Appendix.

Table of Contents

Introduction

• **Pointing** The application, with a trowel, of mortar in between brick or masonry joints; "repointing" refers to removing deteriorated mortar and reapplying a mortar mixture.

At first glance…

From slate roof restorations to minor gutter replacements, from major repointing to simple repainting, this book will guide congregations through the process of managing repair and restoration projects for older buildings. Of course, projects vary widely—according to scope, the size of the congregation, and the building's geographic location, among other factors. Still, there are eight basic steps that every congregation will approach. This book is divided into eight chapters, one for each step.

While the chapters are arranged successively, the book need not be read cover to cover to be helpful. Readers should feel free to read the relevant parts of the text as necessary, skimming ahead or backwards as their needs and interests dictate. Indeed, the repair process generally takes longer than one expects. A congregation may make use of the first two chapters, on identifying problems and developing a project committee, within a few months, but not be ready to use the fifth, on soliciting contractor's bids, for a year.

Reading the chapters

The beginning chapters have been written broadly, to apply to projects of all scopes and sizes. However, in Chapter 3, congregations will decide whether to hire a building consultant, such as a preservation architect, to assist with project planning and management. The decision will have a considerable effect on how the rest of the project is managed. Accordingly, Chapters 4, 5, 7, and 8 are divided into two sections: the first is for congregations working with a consultant, and the second is for congregations working alone. While hiring a consultant is always the best way to go, it may not be practical for some congregations with small-scale repairs and tight budgets. Congregations working alone are advised to read both sections of each chapter. That way, they can follow a professional's example whenever possible, and will understand the expectations of contractors used to working with consultants.

Using supplementary materials

To clarify the differences between congregations working with and without a consultant—and to provide a narrative for understanding the whole repair process—two scenarios are included in the Appendix. In the first scenario, a large congregation hires a preservation architect to prioritize its building's needs and, with her help, completes a project with several components. In the second scenario, a smaller congregation has limited time and money to apply to a badly leaking roof. The congregation works on its own to identify how the roof should be replaced, communicate its expectations to potential contractors, and see the project to completion. The scenarios have been divided into sections based on the book's chapters. While the scenarios

The icon ⊙ indicates that a sample of the document mentioned appears in the Appendix.

represent ideal circumstances—volunteers are enthusiastic, research is comprehensive, and nothing goes very wrong—they will be useful as models and illustrations of how the whole process actually works.

Also included in the Appendix are: sample documents (such as contracts), loosely based on the two scenarios, a glossary, and a list of resources to contact, read, research, or subscribe to. The Resource section will direct readers to basic preservation information, such as the Secretary of the Interior's Standards, as well as Web sites and publications for more managerial topics, such as fundraising.

Basic terminology

• For the sake of simplicity, this book uses the term "congregation" to mean congregation, parish, meeting, clergy, representative of the congregation, owner of the religious institution, or building, property, or project committee. In other words, the congregation is whatever body is responsible for coordinating the repair project. (Project committees are recommended in Chapter 2.)

• "Building consultant" refers to architects, engineers, or building conservators: professionals who work for and represent the congregation, in contrast to contractors. Consultants help the congregation plan and manage repair projects.

• A "contractor" could be a general contractor or an individual or firm with specific expertise, such as a roofer or a mason. Unlike consultants, contractors don't represent the building owner; they represent themselves or their firm through the execution of a construction project.

• "Construction" or "work" refers to the job that the contractor does: the physical activity that changes or fixes the state of the building.

• "Repair project" or "repair" is meant to include repair and restoration work. Restoration usually implies a large-scale capital improvement meant to bring the building close to its original state, while repair can be more routine, like gutter replacement. Still, both types of work require the steps for planning and contracting covered in this book.

A comprehensive glossary of terms encountered in the text appears in the Appendix. Some are also defined in chapter margins.

Acknowledgements

Managing Repair & Restoration Projects *could not have been produced without the following individuals, professionals and staff members, who have given this book its honesty and practicality. We greatly appreciate their contributions of time and expertise. Further, the Landmarks Conservancy would like to deeply thank our financial supporters for their ongoing confidence in the project.*

Professional readers, reviewers, and advisers

John Bero, *Bero Associates Architects,* Rochester, New York

Larry Burda, Sr., *Burda Construction Corp.,* Brooklyn, New York

Franny Eberhart, *Church of the Holy Trinity,* New York, New York

Stephen Facey, *Cathedral of St. John the Divine,* New York, New York

Joan Flanagan, *Joan Flanagan & Associates,* Chicago, Illinois

Ken Follett, *Apple Restoration & Waterproofing,* Brooklyn, New York

John M. Forelle, Esquire, *Simpson Thacher & Bartlett,* New York, New York

Tuomi Forrest, *Partners for Sacred Places,* Philadelphia, Pennsylvania

Wesley Haynes, *New Jersey Historic Trust,* Trenton, New Jersey

Scott Konrad, *Church Insurance,* Avon, Conneticut

Lori E. Lesser, Esquire, *Simpson, Thacher & Bartlett,* New York, New York

The Reverend Doctor Thomas F. Pike, *Calvary/St.George's Episcopal Church, and Landmarks Preservation Commission,* New York, New York

Michael Rebic, *Property Support of the Episcopal Diocese of New York,* New York, New York

Heather Rudge, *Cleveland Restoration Society,* Cleveland, Ohio

Stanley Smith, *Historic Boston Incorporated,* Boston, Massachusetts

Bill Stivale, *Building Conservator,* New York, New York

Neal Vogel, *Inspired Partnerships,* Chicago, Illinois

Kaitsen Woo, *Kaitsen Woo Design & Consulting,* Flushing, New York

Financial supporters

Furthermore, the publication program of The J.M. Kaplan Fund

The Prospect Hill Foundation

Samuel H. Kress Foundation

Landmarks Conservancy Staff Readers

Karen Ansis	Roger P. Lang
Jill Crawford	James J. Mahoney
Ann-Isabel Friedman	Lucretia Norelli
Andrea M. Goldwyn	Jaye Z. Pockriss
Alex Herrera	Peter S. Pockriss

This book was conceived by Ken M. Lustbader, Director of the Landmarks Conservancy's Sacred Sites Program. His extensive experience and sound advice have defined the fundamental aspects of the text.

Peg Breen, President of the Landmarks Conservancy, has given her strong support to the idea, development, and production of this publication.

Written by **Shari P. Goldberg**

Design The Oliphant Press

Chapter 1.

In Chapter 1 readers can learn to:

► Find out about the building's historic designation

► Research the building's history

► Inspect the site

► Contact preservation organizations for assistance

Almost all older buildings suffer from deferred maintenance. When budgets are tight, congregations often postpone basic upkeep projects. Yet delaying minor work often causes major problems: a clogged gutter can eventually lead to serious interior leaks. Buildings require vigilant attention and steady upkeep. The first step in the repair process is the same for every congregation: making a commitment to improving, and then maintaining, the building's condition.

Usually, a sudden calamity turns the congregation's attention to its building. However, a major anniversary, large donation, or simple enthusiasm can be equally encouraging. Once the congregation has committed to the upkeep of the house of worship, a flexible general plan should be identified. The congregation may decide to broadly evaluate the building's condition to prepare for a major restoration. Alternatively, it may want to repair one deteriorated element. Either way, the congregation should begin by understanding the building's history and condition. This will provide a solid background for reference as more detailed plans are made.

► Historic preservation

Congregations with older buildings are usually proud of their structure's history. Their building may have been designated a local landmark, or listed on the State and National Registers of Historic Places. If this is the case, the congregation is probably familiar with the field of historic preservation. If the congregation's older building is not a landmark, but members are committed to its longevity and heritage, they can learn about preservation with this book.

Repairs discussed in the following chapters are expected to be preservation-oriented. They won't all be glamorous restorations, but they should aim to preserve the aesthetics and structures of older architecture. They should be guided by a few key preservation principles, which have been enumerated by the National Parks Service in the Secretary of the Interior's Standards for the Treatment of Historic Properties.

The Secretary of the Interior's Standards are a set of guidelines for preserving, rehabilitating, restoring, and reconstructing culturally and architecturally important older buildings. They recommend repairing rather than replacing older materials, maintaining distinctive details, and, when replacement is necessary, using new materials and techniques that are compatible with the old.

Before embarking on a repair project, the congregation should have a basic familiarity with the Standards (they can be downloaded online or ordered from the National Park Service, as noted under Resources). The Standards will be useful for preliminary planning, to identify types of deterioration and consider potential solutions. Further, any consultant or contractor hired should be familiar with the

- **Permit** Authorization from a municipal agency allowing a specific construction project. One or more permits, issued by agencies such as the Buildings Department or the Landmarks Commission, may be necessary for repair work, depending on local laws and the building's landmark status; congregations should find out about requirements before signing a contract to execute work.

- **As-built drawings** Architectural drawings completed after the construction of a building; these may vary considerably from the original plans.

Standards and willing to employ them. Congregations should also note that most preservation grant programs require that work is done in accordance with the Standards.

Similarly, if a congregation's building is a designated *local* landmark, its work may be required to follow the Standards or other preservation guidelines. Municipal agencies, such as New York City's Landmarks Preservation Commission, often require that landmarked buildings apply for permits for repairs that go beyond routine maintenance. The permitting process helps to ensure that alterations do not damage the building and are made in a historically appropriate way.

By contrast, buildings that have been designated historic by the State Historic Preservation Office (SHPO) will be listed on the State and National Registers of Historic Places, and will not be subject to a permitting process. The State and National Registers are meant to catalogue and honor, not regulate, America's historic sites. (However, if government funding is being applied to a property listed on the Registers, a review may be necessary; the SHPO can provide more information in such cases.) State and National Register listing is often sought by property owners to acknowledge their building's past or make them eligible for preservation grant programs. Interested congregations should contact their SHPO for more information about the application process.

Congregations with locally landmarked buildings should contact their municipal preservation agency to find out about the permitting process. The agency will probably have information about the building's social and architectural history on file, too, which the congregation will want to have on hand. The SHPO will make available their records on State and National Register properties as well.

▶ Research

Finding out about a building's historic designation will provide a foundation for more extensive research. The congregation should seek information that will allow it to plan repairs that are compatible with its structure's history. Its own records will usually provide useful primary information; the local buildings department, library, or historical society may also have relevant materials archived.

Congregations should begin by looking into the building's architectural history and recording when it was built, by whom, and with what materials. The congregation should then try to find the building plans, which show how the building was originally designed, and as-built drawings or old photographs, to see how it was actually constructed. Historic town or insurance maps can also be helpful, providing clues about the building's development in terms of the surrounding community.

Next, the congregation will want to look on-

- **Conditions survey** A comprehensive, holistic evaluation of a building, prepared by a preservation consultant, that identifies its features and materials as well as its deficiencies and their causes. Generally based on visual inspection but can include physical probes if necessary. The survey report includes recommendations for repair projects, prioritized by urgency, and, usually, cost estimates for the work.

- **Flashing** A thin waterproof material placed to prevent water penetration and/or provide drainage, especially at roof corners, between a roof and wall, and over exterior door openings and windows.

- **Building envelope** The primary exterior planes enclosing a building that protect it from water infiltration, including the exterior walls, roof, foundation, windows, and doors.

site to establish a history of building repairs. This information is most likely to be found in a dusty file drawer or old meeting record book. Asking the following questions will yield valuable background information: when was the last time a repair project took place? What was it? How much did it cost? Was a building consultant used? If a building consultant was hired in the past, some kind of conditions survey may be in place—which can be a useful tool for understanding deterioration and choosing repair projects. More specific questions should also be considered: what alterations have been made to the building, and when? What materials were used at that time? While considering past changes, the congregation may want to think about the future, too. Are there new programs that will require additional space? Is the congregation interested in upgrading a sound system, or installing architectural lighting? Although these last items may not be included in a repair project, having them in mind can assist in budgeting and long-term planning.

▶ Inspection

Next, the congregation will need to physically inspect the building and identify what needs work. It may be helpful to do the inspection with a custodian who has access to difficult-to-reach places and can explain recent maintenance performed. The goal of the inspection is to develop two lists. One will have basic mainte-

nance items to be funded from an operating budget, such as fixing gutters or painting wooden window frames. The other will comprise major repair projects that will require a separate capital budget.

When a major project is identified, the area should be evaluated as thoroughly as possible. Congregations should always aim to find the source of the deterioration, which must be repaired before more cosmetic work is undertaken. For instance, if a water stain on an interior plaster wall looks like it must be repaired, the congregation will want to find the origin of the leak. Ultimately, it may have been caused by a combination of exterior problems: deteriorated shingles and flashing and clogged gutters, for instance. In that case, repairs to the building exterior—known as the envelope—would take priority over those to the interior wall.

After a thorough investigation has been completed, small-scale maintenance projects should be set on a calendar with a plan for accomplishing them, either through volunteer labor, a staff custodian, or by hiring workers or a contractor. The congregation should then address its list of capital repair projects. To do so, it will want to form a project committee as discussed in Chapter 2.

The long haul

Repair and restoration projects take a long time—up to a full year or even two from conception to completion. Most congregations don't realize that planning the project will take more time than the actual construction. Once the congregation has decided to hire a consultant, for instance, it may need to allow two months between the time that proposals are solicited and submitted. The consultant's conditions survey can take another two months to complete, and then the consultant's recommendations must be assimilated by the congregation. Next, plans and specifications will need to be developed, and contractors' bids requested...all of which can take up to six months. Of course, group decision-making always takes a long time, which is why a congregation that doesn't hire a consultant should still anticipate several months of planning.

The good news is that the congregation won't be on-call for an entire year without a break. In fact, there is some downtime in the process, especially while waiting for work to be completed by a consultant or contractor. During these gaps, the congregation will want to focus on publicity and, often, fundraising, to maintain strong public support for its work.

▶ Help from preservation organizations

As the congregation gets a sense of its repair plans, it may want to consult preservation organizations for advice.

The Landmarks Conservancy, for example, which produced this book, is a private nonprofit that provides financial, technical, and educational assistance to owners of historic properties in New York State. Organizations with similar programs exist in other states too, and some counties, cities, or towns have their own preservation groups. Depending on the group's mission, it may provide information about the repair process, recommendations of qualified preservation architects or other building consultants, referrals for experienced contractors, advice on appropriate materials and techniques, and sometimes grants.

Contact information for State Historic Preservation Offices, which can refer congregations to private local or state organizations, is provided under Resources.

Chapter 2.

Assigning Responsibility

In Chapter 2 readers can learn to:

▶ Gain confidence as potential project leaders

▶ Set up a project committee

▶ Define the committee's responsibilities

▶ Delegate duties

▶ Consider fundraising

Repair projects demand a lot of attention, almost from the moment that the congregation considers them. It is recommended that congregations form a dedicated project committee early in the planning process. Some congregations will already have a building or property committee in place; still, they should consider designating a separate project committee for major repairs.

Project committees must take on a significant amount of work. They are responsible for the welfare of both the physical building and the congregation as repairs are made. This entails managing inspections, construction, and maintenance, in addition to representing the interests of the congregation to consultants or contractors. No doubt these tasks will appear daunting to novice or new committee members. Regardless of the work to be done or the community involved, however, a good committee needs only concerned and motivated volunteers to be successful.

▶ Gaining confidence

Most members of religious institutions don't feel totally comfortable with the subject of building repairs. They may know their building's history and be able to perceive what works and what doesn't, but they rarely feel confident about embarking on a repair plan or speaking to contractors. Again, potential committee members shouldn't be discouraged by a lack of experience. Hundreds of project committees without technical expertise have taken on thousands of repair projects. To succeed, a committee needs a commitment to the building's longevity, a willingness to learn, an ability to communicate with the congregation, and a sensible and organized decision-making structure.

▶ Setting up a project committee

Identifying a leader

The project committee will need a leader. Someone with building-related experience may be a good choice; for example, one who has recently made repairs to a historic home or an architect, engineer, or contractor. But someone with good communication and management skills is equally fit for the job. The leader should form a committee with anywhere from one to ten other members, depending on the size of the congregation.

Setting goals

When motivated volunteers are found, a committee structure should be set. First, members should define a goal. Having a goal will unite the individuals in the group and allow them to discern what work is and is not appropriate for them to undertake. The goal will vary according to the committee; it may aim to spend one week planning or it may look towards completing a project. Of course, goals can shift and additional goals can be added as work gets underway. One or all of these might be named as an initial goal:

- *To repair the roof within the next six months.*
- *To understand the building's history and use the Secretary of the Interior's Standards to choose appropriate materials with which to repair it.*
- *To get a specialist's opinion on restoring the stained glass windows.*
- *To provide a healthy, dry, safe environment for all programming.*

Defining rules

Next, organizational rules should be developed. These need not be strict by-laws, but a basic structure for reaching goals should be established. Duties may be assigned to individual members, or dates set for future meetings. Here is one example:

> *The committee will meet once every two weeks, on Thursday evenings, while the project is underway. Meetings will be moderated by the committee chairperson and will require progress reports from each member. One member will meet with the fundraising committee on alternate weeks.*

▶ Responsibilities of the committee

After its structure has been established, the project committee should expect to work with four other people or groups of people: the congregation, the clergy, consultants, and contractors. The tasks to be accomplished in relation to each are outlined below.

Congregation

The project committee must keep the congregation aware, informed, and invested in the repair work. If the congregation is kept in the dark, it won't understand—and usually won't support—the need for work. By contrast, a well-informed group is often willing to volunteer at events and solicit donations from community members. Plentiful, positive communication is the key to building enthusiasm and should be one of the committee's first priorities. Here are some ideas for publicizing the plans and work of the project committee:

- *Start a buildings and grounds column in the congregational newsletter.*
- *Start a buildings and grounds newsletter.*
- *Develop a promotional video or Web site about the building's needs and the committee's plans.*
- *Announce updates as often as possible; in weekly services, for example.*
- *Designate a committee contact person who is willing to discuss repair plans with interested congregants.*
- *If possible, have the clergy make his/her support for the project known to the congregation.*
- *Write a letter explaining the committee's plans for the next few months, to be mailed or emailed to the congregation.*
- *Post notices or signs explaining the project plans (illustrations are especially helpful) in all highly trafficked areas: on the exterior of the*

building as well as inside in bathrooms, classrooms, and spaces rented to outside organizations.

- *If a religious school is in the complex, ask teachers to announce the plans to their students.*
- *Plan to provide "hard-hat tours" of the construction site while the work is being done.*
- *Send a press release to the local newspaper about photo and article opportunities while the building is under construction.*

Clergy

The role of the clergy in institutional administration varies among denominations and individual congregations. The clergy should be involved with repair projects in whatever capacity s/he is comfortable. That said, the vocal support of the clergy can be invaluable. If the clergy does not sit on the project committee, s/he should be kept well-informed of its plans and decisions and encouraged to discuss them with congregants.

Consultants

One of the committee's major responsibilities involves hiring and working with a suitable building consultant. When it is ready for this step, the committee will need to: find consultants who have had experience with historic religious buildings, contact consultants to request proposals and set up site visits, give basic tours

of the property, review consultants' proposals and select the most appropriate one, make the building available for the consultant's assessment, and meet with the consultant to review his/her assessments and recommendations. As noted previously, some congregations will not hire a consultant. The committee should make this decision carefully after reading Chapter 3.

Contractors

Eventually, all congregations will need to communicate with the contractor and make logistic arrangements to accommodate the work and workers. If a congregation hires a building consultant to manage the project, the consultant will handle much of the communication and negotiation. If a congregation is working alone, the committee will have a considerable task list, including: obtaining referrals for qualified contractors, soliciting bids, negotiating an appropriate contract, overseeing the actual construction, and approving payment requests.

Delegation and other duties

Many of the duties described above can be best accomplished by delegation. For instance, one congregant may be the contact person for the clergy, and another for consultants and contractors. A committee member with good writing skills may be the one to develop a project newsletter.

Additional responsibilities of the committee,

which may be delegated, are:

- *Scheduling regular building inspections to monitor problems and notice when something requires attention.*
- *Learning about the repair process (by reading books like this!).*
- *Consulting the institution's administration and legal counsel before signing contracts and issuing checks.*
- *Guiding staff to maintain work after it has been completed.*
- *Planning for future repair projects.*
- *Working with or forming a fundraising committee to make building repairs a priority.*
- *Assisting the fundraising committee in the preparation of grant applications or other funding requests.*

Fundraising

These last duties are crucial. A congregation must always have sufficient funding in hand before signing a contract with a consultant or contractor. As it begins planning, therefore, the committee must know how much money is available and have a sense of its fundraising capacity. Its financial situation will affect whether or not a consultant is hired, how many repair projects are executed, and what kind of publicity will be sought.

If the congregation has no fundraising body in place, it may be necessary to designate a fundraising leader or form a fundraising com-

mittee. Many congregations embark on multi-year capital campaigns to raise money for building repairs. Some even hire a fundraising consultant to assess the congregation's giving ability or plan events. This guidebook will not focus on fundraising—others have done so comprehensively—but project committee members should be aware of its importance. Fundraising resources can be found in the Appendix.

It's not over until…

Potential committee members should be aware that the repair process is rarely a one-shot deal. Even the most basic repair project, undertaken with or without a consultant, can take months or years from start to finish. Further, in between projects, the committee may have little to do, until it plunges back into building-related tasks. In order to preserve its momentum, the committee should aim to keep up with its basic duties (communication with the congregation and fundraising committee, for instance) at all times. Rotating committee seats is another way to keep energy and enthusiasm high. As with any volunteer organization, accurate paper records should be kept to maintain the committee's collective knowledge.

Chapter 3.

Working with Consultants

One of the building committee's first tasks is to hire a consultant, or decide to plan and manage the repair on its own. The Landmarks Conservancy strongly recommends that congregations hire a building consultant, such as a preservation architect, for all restoration projects. A consultant is especially important if the building has several expensive problems, and none is obviously the most urgent. However, if the congregation has completed a thorough inspection and identified one small-scale repair to undertake, a consultant may not be necessary. Congregations should read on to determine whether or not a consultant must be hired.

▶ The value of a consultant

In general, the consultant will help the congregation approach its building comprehensively and with professional expertise. S/he will work with—and for—the congregation to evaluate the structure, plan repairs, hire an experienced contractor, and administer the construction contract.

The consultant's number one tool is the conditions survey. By surveying the building, the consultant will be able to identify the building's problems and prioritize necessary repairs. Then, once the congregation is ready to pursue its first repair project, s/he will generate a technical description of the job and help procure a contract with a qualified contractor. The consultant's involvement will help ensure that all work done is appropriate to the historic structure, and that the contractor executes repairs thoughtfully and adequately.

▶ Types of consultants

Most congregations will hire a preservation architect as their primary building consultant. An architect may need to call in a specialist, such as a structural engineer or building conservator, but will remain the team leader. The specialists will serve as subconsultants and the architect will interpret their conclusions to inform his/her own recommendations.

In certain situations, a congregation may decide to hire an engineer or building conservator as the primary consultant. A structural engineer may be a good choice when the building is known to have a specific structural problem. Alternatively, a few building conservators have established a niche as consultants for religious institutions, overseeing the planning and implementation of repair projects. In general, however, hiring a preservation architect won't be a mistake; if certain aspects of the project need additional expertise, a specialist can always be employed.

The following basic distinctions will help congregations determine who to hire, or to understand the types of subconsultants who may ultimately be involved in their projects.

What architects do

Preservation architects tend to make good building consultants because of their background in project planning and their experience with traditional construction techniques and materials. Architects help clients analyze the needs of their buildings and then generate documents explaining the work required to meet those needs.

Congregations usually use two contracts in the course of working with an architect. The first is for the planning phase, or conditions survey, in which the architect evaluates the building conditions, prioritizes the work necessary, and helps to identify an appropriate repair project. After the congregation has fundraised and is ready to execute the project, a second contract is drawn. The second contract includes preparation of construction documents, assistance in the bidding and negotiation process, and administration of the contracts between client and contractor. Typically, the congregation uses the same architect for both contracts; however, if problems arise during planning, or a long period of time elapses between contracts, it may opt to hire someone new for construction.

For both contracts, many architects will use the American Institute of Architects (AIA) owner-architect agreement. This is a standard, comprehensive document, generally perceived to be fair to both parties.

What engineers do

Engineers are trained in a methodic problem-solving process. Engineers specialize in a variety of disciplines from chemistry to electricity; two types of engineers that regularly work on buildings are structural engineers and M.E.P. (mechanical, electrical, and plumbing) engineers. Structural engineers focus on building structures; with older religious buildings, they commonly confront overstressed trusses or damaged foundations. M.E.P. engineers deal with building systems, such as heating, ventilation, air conditioning, power, and fire safety systems.

What conservators do

Building conservators work with historic buildings and the materials they comprise. Like engineers, building conservators specialize in different areas. Some primarily evaluate and test historic materials, such as masonry and paint; others serve as preservation consultants for architectural firms; others plan and oversee construction projects. Depending on a conservation firm's expertise, a conservator could be called to evaluate a building's existing condition, research its history, generate lab analyses of certain material components, or develop techniques for specified repairs.

In-house professionals

Congregations sometimes consider hiring a member of the congregation, or an affiliate of the institution, who will work at a discount. Hiring in-house is generally not recommended. While the initial easy relationship may tempt committees, a working arrangement can be difficult to set among parties that usually interact informally. Compensation and the donation of in-kind services can be problematic if they are not explicitly defined before the project begins.

However, the advice and opinions of in-house professionals can be very valuable to the building committee. The committee should let them know that their participation is welcome.

▶ Hiring consultants

Once the congregation has chosen a type of consultant and has a list of referrals, it should begin prequalification (this is fully explained at the end of the chapter). Those with sufficient experience and good recommendations should be asked to submit a proposal for a conditions survey. This request for proposals● is different from a bid solicitation (given to contractors) in that the congregation is asking the consultant to help define and develop a plan for the work. The congregation should aim to describe its expectations as specifically as possible, so that the consultant's proposals are generally similar and within the same price range. That way, the proposals will be relatively simple to evaluate and compare. The congregation may develop a formal, written request for proposals, or it may convey its request in a telephone call, visit, or simple letter.

Before hiring a consultant who seems experienced, friendly, and fair, the congregation should verify that his/her insurance is appropriate for the job. In general, this will include professional liability insurance, commercial general liability insurance, workers' compensation (unless the consultant is a sole practitioner), and automobile insurance for vehicles owned, not owned, and hired.

The selected consultant will prepare a contract for his/her services. At that time, the congregation can request that it be listed as "additionally insured" under the consultant's general liability insurance. When a contractor is hired, both the consultant and the congregation can be listed as additionally insured under the contractor's commercial general liability insurance. More information about the congregation's own insurance can be found in Chapter 4.

▶ When it's OK to work alone

The cost of hiring a consultant may seem prohibitive to congregations on tight budgets, especially as they consider the cost of the contractor's work. Fundraising in order to afford a consultant is desirable; still, some congregations face problems too immediate or resources too scarce to make a campaign feasible. In such cases, it may be acceptable to hire an experienced contractor directly—if the identified project is simple and self-contained.

Projects that may be adequately executed without a consultant should have a fairly obvious problem and a fairly obvious solution. They should be limited to one building element (such as a small roof repair). They should not be part of a larger project, nor should they be one repair among several competing for attention and funds. They should not be full restoration projects, such as slate roof replacements or comprehensive masonry work. In general, they should not include replacement of historic building materials. In other words, if the project is anything more major or comprehensive than a rou-

• **Request for proposals** A document describing work, usually a conditions survey, that a congregation wants done by a building consultant. In turn, the consultant will submit a proposed method and price for completing the job.

• **Prequalification** The process of investigating the qualifications of prospective consultants or contractors *before* proposals or bids are solicited.

tine repair or replacement, the congregation should always find the means to hire a consultant. Otherwise, the congregation risks undertaking an inappropriate repair that may lead to further, more complicated, and more expensive problems.

Congregations may have anticipated making one small repair at first, but should be willing to expand the scope if circumstances demand it. Congregations unsure about the complexity of a planned project should contact the Landmarks Conservancy (or another preservation organization) for advice on whether hiring a consultant is necessary. They may also consider hiring a preservation architect to perform a walk-through inspection, instead of a full survey, of the whole building or one problem area. The architect is usually paid hourly for such work; a member of the congregation can record the architect's observations and use them as a basis for repair planning.

If no consultant is involved at all, the congregation must engage in a thorough planning process as described in Chapters 4 and 5. It should be sure to hire a qualified, experienced contractor as well.

▶ Before hiring anyone

Congregations should always try to prequalify consultants or contractors before soliciting bids or proposals●. Prequalification is the process of determining in advance that someone has the qualifications necessary to do the job. Prequalification saves the congregation time by ensuring that it only considers capable consultants and contractors.

One important aspect of prequalification involves identifying consultants and contractors with significant preservation experience and supporting references. Such expertise is somewhat rare. Most architects, for example, are trained broadly in building design but haven't been exposed to traditional construction techniques, or the care older buildings require. Contractors, too, may have done lots of roofs but never a historic cedar shingle one. Congregations might also look to prequalify those who have previously worked with religious institutions, both because the building elements are unique and because a building committee is not a typical client. Certain accommodations may be required—such as dealing with an entire committee instead of one owner, or stopping work for an unanticipated funeral.

To start making a list of prequalified people, congregations should seek referrals from preservation organizations, denominational offices, or neighboring congregations. Potential consultants or contractors should be asked to submit a list of contacts for their recently-completed preservation projects; the contacts should be called and asked about issues like responsiveness and timeliness, as well as their general satisfaction with the work performed. If possible, the

Project managers

Someone on the building repair team will need to take responsibility for overall coordination of the project. This point person is often called a "project manager." The project manager will communicate with contractors, receive bids, oversee construction, and approve invoices and payments.

Congregations working alone will need to appoint a project manager from the building committee. However, hired building consultants will often act as the project manager. Most architects include "contract administration" in their second contracts. This is an industry term for overseeing construction and execution of the owner-contractor agreement. Yet architects offer varying degrees of oversight within "contract administration." Some will make periodic visits to the site and approve payments, but will not monitor the work intensely. Congregations should review their expectations for management and administration with their building consultant to prevent confusion. Congregations should also note that a separate consultant—an owner's representative, clerk of the works, construction manager, or someone called simply a project manager—is sometimes hired to specifically perform management tasks. This usually takes place on large-scale, comprehensive, or new construction projects.

More on contract administration and project management can be found in Chapter 8.

congregation should visit their sites.

Congregations will then want to schedule on-site interviews with the most promising consultants or contractors. No cost is involved with such meetings. They are an opportunity to assess the experience, approachability, and pricing policy of the interviewees. At this point, the congregation may want to discuss professional liability and general insurance. Contractors in particular, but also architects and engineers, should also be able to provide proof of in-state licensing.

Actual proposals or bids should only be solicited from those professionals whose experience and personality seem compatible with the congregation's anticipated project. It is advisable to seek proposals from at least three prequalified professionals for all job openings.

Chapter 4.

Planning the Work

In Chapter 4 readers can learn to:

▶ Work with a consultant to assess the building's conditions, prioritize necessary repairs, and develop a phase of work to undertake

▶ Research methods and materials for an identified project without a consultant

• **Master plan** A document or set of plans proposing a change in the design or use of a building; may be undertaken by congregations wanting to enlarge their building or reconfigure its use of space.

After a congregation has formed a committee and hired a consultant (if one is to be hired), in-depth project planning can begin. The congregation will now focus on establishing the details of the project in preparation for soliciting contractors' bids.

Congregations who have hired a consultant to do a conditions survey won't have much to do, initially. The consultant will inspect the building and determine what repairs are needed. The consultant will then develop techniques for making the repairs, and will start to establish an order in which they should be done. The congregation will be involved with confirming priorities and selecting one project, a repair or group of repairs that is both urgent and affordable.

A congregation working alone will need to undertake inspections, evaluations, and research at this point. The committee will already have generally defined the project. Planning will thus consist of discovering the best methods and materials for completing the work.

▶ Planning with a building consultant

The conditions survey◉ is the ultimate planning tool. First, the consultant preparing the survey is objective; s/he won't recommend more work than is necessary. Second, the survey analysis is holistic, taking all of the building into account. Third, out of all the consultant's findings, s/he will produce a streamlined document. This will usually prioritize the work items, so that a congregation knows it will have to do the roof

before it considers the masonry, the masonry before the interior…et cetera. Conditions surveys usually contain cost estimates as well, which are invaluable for yearly budgeting and fundraising campaigns.

Surveys may deal with the entire building, or they may concentrate on a specific area or element; the roof, for instance, or the sanctuary. They do not, however, include space analysis or future design planning. Such evaluation is part of a master plan, which is considerably more expensive than a standard conditions survey.

To undertake a survey, the building consultant will make several visits to the site. Depending on his/her expertise, other specialists may be called in; for example, an architect may bring a conservator to analyze mortar or a structural engineer to examine beams. Then the primary consultant will analyze the collected information.

The findings of the survey will be presented to the congregation. The consultant will work with the congregation to plan a schedule for completing the recommended repairs. Instead of planning to execute them one by one, "phases," or groups of repairs, will be developed.

In defining the first phase, the congregation should consider the building's most urgent needs, its fundraising capacity, and its long-term repair plans. In addition to urgent items, the first phase may also include easy-to-do maintenance items (such as cleaning out gutters), or a

• **Plans** Also called drawings. Documents generated by an architect or other building consultant to graphically describe the project to the contractor. Almost always accompanied and explained by written technical specifications. Together, the plans and specifications form the construction documents of the bid package or contract.

• **Specifications** Written by the architect (or other building consultant) to explain the exact technical requirements of the work to the contractor. Illustrated by the plans.

small project to encourage future fundraising, like a sample cleaning. The remaining phases may be set out with anticipated dates for completion (for example, within five years), or without dates, to be completed as funds become available.

It is important to understand that the survey is a planning document—it can't be used to solicit bids. The consultant will need to prepare plans and specifications before contractors can be approached (more about this in Chapter 5). Further, cost estimates are useful for establishing fundraising goals, but they should be confirmed when the congregation is actually ready to execute the work.

▶ Planning without a building consultant
Congregations working alone shouldn't require a conditions survey to determine necessary work, since the project will already have been identified. At this point, the congregation should focus on understanding the parameters of the problem and choosing methods and materials for its solution. At the conclusion of the planning phase, the congregation should be ready to generate a project description that will be used to solicit contractors' bids.

First, the congregation should perform a thorough inspection of the area to be repaired. The condition of each material there should be recorded. The congregation will also want to get a sense of which materials can be repaired and

which will need to be replaced. For example, a congregation planning an asphalt roof replacement will want to note the condition and color of the shingles, how they have deteriorated or otherwise aged, and what shape the surrounding materials—sheathing beneath, flashing and gutters around—are in.

If the congregation notices serious problems in other areas of the building, it probably should not proceed without hiring a consultant. Otherwise, it may complete a repair only to realize that the source of the deterioration hasn't been addressed, and will continue to cause damage.

Once the inspection has been made, the congregation will want help interpreting its findings. People to talk to and other resources are listed below. In addition to general information—such as approximate costs, recommended contractors, and the estimated duration of the project—detailed information on products and techniques should be sought. Indeed, anything that the lay committee isn't certain about should be subjected to a professional opinion. Advice on appropriate measures for historic properties, cost-effective procedures, and materials with simple maintenance may be especially useful.

Although this step may seem intimidating, it is the best way to develop a well-defined plan. Congregations shouldn't worry that their inquiries are simplistic; good advisers will respect their interest and earnestness. The following organizations, individuals, and publications are recommended. Contact information for many may be found under Resources.

Nonprofit preservation organizations that offer technical assistance

Depending on the scope of the program, on-site evaluations may be available. Otherwise, a staff member may be willing to discuss the project and suggest a course of action.

Books, magazines, pamphlets, and journals

Several publications address the subject of taking care of old buildings, some of which are particularly geared towards laypeople. The National Parks Service has produced over 40 Preservation Briefs, on topics that range from controlling moisture to replacing roofs. *Inspecting and Maintaining Religious Properties*, published by the New York Landmarks Conservancy, explains how to evaluate different building components. A number of magazines also focus on older buildings. *Common Bond*, the Landmarks Conservancy's journal, is specifically written for laypeople repairing historic houses of worship. It covers both administrative and technical issues. Finally, trade-oriented publications can be helpful for learning about specific products or techniques.

Contractors

The congregation may want to approach contractors, not for a formal bid, but for a proposal on how they would fix the problem at hand. Comparing the proposals of several different contractors will give the congregation a sense of the materials and techniques available to it.

Local denominational or adjudicatory groups

These bodies may offer financial or technical resources, or may be able to direct congregations to others who have successfully undertaken similar projects.

In-house human resources

If a congregant has had experience repairing historic buildings, s/he may assist by offering advice. If the project is outside his/her scope of expertise, s/he may be willing to turn to others in the field.

Other congregations who have received a consultant's advice

If a neighboring institution has completed a large project, its leadership may have helpful recommendations.

Home improvement or repair stores

These places can help a congregation to compare the types of materials available for solving the building's problem. Some retail establishments even provide information about when to

Project budgeting

Because a conditions survey includes cost estimates for recommended repair work, it is a useful tool for planning fundraising campaigns. Congregations will be able to anticipate how much they need to undertake their first phase of work and how much will need to be raised for future projects.

The cost estimates may not be as straightforward as they seem, however, as they cover only the cost of construction. The congregation must also anticipate paying the consultant for preparing plans and specifications and for bidding and contract administration. The total project cost often demands considerable fundraising.

Since the plans and specifications must be completed first, a congregation may be tempted to have the consultant generate them and then to take on fundraising for the actual work. But such an approach isn't always wise. It may take years, once the plans and specifications have been completed, until the funding is in place for construction. By that point, the building's condition may have changed, requiring new plans to be drawn. Also, it is unfair to set up the project with the consultant if it won't be put out to bid for a long time.

In short, congregations should fundraise for plans and specifications, contract administration, and construction all at once. It's OK to undertake a conditions survey and then pause to fundraise for the recommended repairs. But it doesn't make sense to have plans and specifications developed and then take a long fundraising break. Of course, the congregation must never sign a contract with any firm without having the funding in hand to execute it fully.

replace elements such as roofs or how to perform inspections. They won't all be well-versed in historic buildings, though, so the congregation should make sure that it accepts only applicable recommendations.

The internet

Information on materials, comparable to that found in a home improvement store, is often available online. Materials manuals, repair techniques, and preservation publications may also be accessible on the Web.

The congregation will want to collect information and advice until it feels confident defining the repair project in detail. In the next chapter, the congregation will record the scope and specifications of the project for contractors to bid on. It will therefore want to be sure that it understands and is certain about all aspects of the job. Before proceeding, the congregation may want to review the following questions: is this a thorough solution to our problem? Will it be long-lasting? Does it take into account the historic nature of the property? Have all the materials involved been chosen thoughtfully? Will a contractor's bid fall within our budget? Are there still many unknowns about what needs to be done or how the work will turn out?

If the answer to all but the last question is yes, the congregation has probably completed its planning work.

Chapter 5.

Soliciting Contractors' Bids

In Chapter 5 readers can learn:

▶ How a consultant prepares a bid package

▶ How to generate a bid package without a consultant

• **Bid package** A set of documents used to solicit contractors' bids. In addition to describing the scope of work with a written statement, or with plans and specifications, they may include: pricing forms, instructions to bidders, qualification forms, non-collusion affidavits, and other addenda.

• **Scope of work** A description of the project to be executed.

The congregation's project will need to be fully articulated in order to solicit contractor's bids. Contractors need to understand both the scope of the work and how their bids for it should be submitted. The congregation should present this information in a bid package. The more specific its scope and submission requirements, the better. Specific bid packages yield bids that can be easily compared.

If the congregation is working with a building consultant, the consultant will prepare plans and specifications as part of a comprehensive bid package. If the congregation is not working with a building consultant, it should provide contractors with a written scope of work and the preferred format for bid submissions. All congregations should be sure to solicit bids from prequalified contractors. Reviewing the components of a contract in Chapter 6 may be helpful as the package is developed.

▶ The consultant's bid package

After a building consultant helps to define the first phase of work, the congregation usually fundraises until it is ready to execute it. The congregation then hires the consultant to take on new responsibilities: preparing a bid package with plans and specifications, managing the bidding process, negotiating with contractors, and administering the contract.

The consultant's bid package is centered around the plans and technical specifications.

Plans are measured drawings that illustrate how the project is to be executed. Specifications accompany the plans, explaining them in words and indicating precise materials, weights, and techniques to be used. Although a less detailed scope of work may also be included in the bid package, the plans and specifications function as instructions for the work. They will be cited as part of the contract once it is signed. In addition, depending on municipal policy, plans and specifications may need to be submitted to the local buildings department, landmarking authority, or architectural review board.

Along with the plans and specifications, the consultant will prepare documents explaining the preferred format for bid submissions. These will often include a form with spaces for the cost of different components of the job, to be filled out by the contractor, which will be used to analyze and compare the bids received.

The bid package may request that the contractor include alternates—parts of the project which may be added to the core scope of work. Alternates are a convenient way to price extra parts of the project that the congregation is not sure it can afford. For instance, a consultant may request 16-ounce copper flashing in the specifications and an alternate price for 20-ounce copper flashing. An alternate may describe a larger project as well, such as replacing an entire roof rather than a portion of one. Alternates are almost always related to the main scope of work.

Finally, the bid package includes logistic information about bid submission: how, when, and where bids should be submitted, the type of contract that will ultimately be used (usually the American Institute of Architects, or AIA, owner-contractor agreement), and insurance and permit requirements. In addition, the consultant may choose to include a non-collusion affidavit, to protect the congregation from price-fixing, or a qualification form◉, which requests a listing of the contractor's relevant experience.

The consultant will have contractors pick up the bid package and review it. S/he will then schedule a pre-bid meeting, when the contractors can walk through the building and ask site-specific questions. As the property owner, a member of the building committee should be present; this is a good chance to get a sense of the contractors' approachability and professionalism. The deadline for bid submissions will follow the site visit.

▶ Soliciting bids without a consultant

A congregation's bid package◉ won't be as professional as a consultant's, but it can still be comprehensive. The congregation should start by writing down its scope of work. Based on the information gleaned in the planning process, this should be a specific description of what the repair is and how the congregation wants it executed. For instance, here is a sample scope of work for a basic asphalt roof replacement:

Replace existing asphalt shingles with new, 40-year architectural asphalt shingles. Replace deteriorated flashing with 20-ounce copper and sheathing, as necessary.

The written scope of work should contain as much detail as possible. If the one above did not specify 40-year architectural asphalt shingles, one contractor might have proposed 40-year shingles and another 20-year shingles. Comparing their prices would be difficult, and the congregation might have had to do more research to choose the better shingle. By being specific in the first place, the congregation will receive proposals only for the type of shingle it wants.

After establishing the scope, the congregation will need to set a format and procedure for bid submissions. The bid package should note a deadline for submissions and a contact person to whom the bids should be sent, and should enumerate any additional documents that bids must include, such as proof of insurance. Congregations should also consider requesting bids that break down the cost of each material; they will allow the congregation to determine which contractor's labor is the least expensive and to demand that contractors explain high materials costs. The next chapter outlines the different components of contracts. It may be helpful in anticipating contractors' bids and generating an appropriate package.

Bid packages should only be given to pre-qualified contractors (as per page 20). The congregation will want to follow up with contractors by scheduling visits to the site. During these visits, the congregation may want to interview the contractors. A pre-bid meeting is a good way to judge whether the contractor seems receptive and interested in the project. Congregations should note that not all contractors will submit bids in response to the bid package.

The bids received are likely to be a one-page letter or form. They will be signed by the contractor and, once signed by the congregation, will become a contract. Prior to signing a bid, the congregation may wish to read through the American Institute of Architects (AIA) owner-contractor agreement, which is generally employed when an architect is involved with a project (AIA contact information is available under Resources). It may be useful for determining that the contractor has covered basic contractual terms fairly. Chapters 6 and 7 will assist with such evaluation as well.

Chapter 6.

Understanding the Contract

In Chapter 6 readers can learn about:

▶ Scope of work

▶ Timing

▶ Site precautions

▶ Obtaining permits

▶ Pricing methods

▶ Payment schedules

▶ Insurance

A bid responding to a congregation without a consultant will probably be a one-page letter or simple form◉. A bid responding to a consultant's bid package will include more detailed information as requested. Still, certain basic elements should be found in all proposals. These elements, listed below, are important parts of the contract. As an accepted bid is the basis for a contract, congregations can use this chapter to verify that bids received are complete. This chapter will also help congregations working alone determine what to include in their bid packages.

Identification

The contract must include the name, address, and phone number of the contractor, prospective client, and the premises to be worked on.

Scope of work

The contractor's expression of the scope must reflect the congregation's, as set in its bid package. Thus it may either be basic, expressed in a few detailed sentences, or may comprise plans and specifications.

Timing

A start date and the amount of time the job will take must appear in the contract. It is advisable that congregations request the addition of a timing clause that allows for possible special scheduling—canceling a day's work for a funeral, for example. Such a clause can allow the con-

gregation to halt a day's work with twelve hours' notice to the contractor. Congregations should note that construction season is usually limited to temperate weather; in the northeastern United States, from March to October.

Site provisions

Congregations will want the following provisions included if they are expected of the contractor: site clean up, following fire safety regulations and precautions during construction, making efforts to decrease pollution, and recycling appropriate materials. Regulations about parking, utility usage, and work hours should also be set forth.

Municipal permits or reviews

Although the responsibility of procuring permits falls on the building owner, many consultants or contractors will obtain them as part of the contract. Construction permits may be required by a municipal buildings department or by a local landmarking agency. Congregations should always verify whether permits or reviews are required by calling the relevant agencies. (If government funding is being used for a State and/or National Register-listed property, a State review may be necessary; congregations in this situation should contact their local State Historic Preservation Office—listed under Resources—for further information.)

• **Retainage** A portion (usually 10%) withheld from progress payments to the contractor until the job has been completely accepted by the owner (and building consultant if applicable). The accumulated retainage is paid with the last and final payment.

Pricing

There are a few different methods for determining and presenting the final cost of the work. It is recommended that congregations request a lump sum for the entire project with a breakdown of the cost of each material to be used. The congregation should define units for each material, such as a square of shingle (or an hour of work), so that the submissions will be consistent. An example of how cost breakdowns may be analyzed appears in the next chapter. Congregations should always remember that consistency in bids makes for easy comparisons and, ultimately, bid selection.

Payment schedules

In addition to stating what the client will pay, the contract defines when the client will pay it. Payment is usually made progressively, at intervals, but schedules vary. For instance, contracts for larger projects may define a series of dates on which the contractor will be paid; the amount due will reflect the percentage of work completed at that time. For smaller projects, the contractor may require a deposit and will then let the congregation know when the job is 25%, 50%, and fully completed, with payment due accordingly.

All progressive payment contracts should provide for retainage. Retainage allows the client to withhold a certain amount, usually 10%, from each payment made. The total amount of the retainage is paid to the contractor when the job is completed and the congregation has received verification that the contractor's bills have been paid. Retainage helps to ensure that the contracting company will complete the work; otherwise, it stands to lose not only its final payment but the accumulated retainage. Retainage also provides the client with leverage for demanding that any unsatisfactory work be corrected.

Warranties

Most contracts include a warranty for the contractor's workmanship. The warranty period is typically one year but may be up to five. If the congregation finds the contractor's work to be inadequate during that time, the contractor is obligated to correct the problem at its own expense. Appropriate problems for warranty correction include improper work techniques or installation of poor materials. Errors or deficiencies in the plans or specifications are not covered by a contractor's warranty. Further, the warranty is only valid as long as the contractor remains in business. As in most other warranties, owner-caused problems, improper maintenance, and natural disasters are not covered.

In addition to the contractor's warranty, most materials come with a manufacturer's warranty. The congregation should be sure that the contractor provides a copy of the manufacturer's warranty for any materials used, preferably attached to the contract for reference. If a material under warranty fails within its guaranteed time, the congregation should contact the manufacturer. Congregations should note that the manufacturer's warranty is only valid if the contractor is trained (in some cases, licensed) to install the product. Contractors should provide proof of such aptitude along with the warranty.

Insurance

The contract should contain a section that addresses the contracting firm's insurance. Contractors should be expected to hold insurance for its own firm, workers, and equipment; commercial general liability insurance; workers' compensation insurance; and automobile liability insurance.

When soliciting bids, the congregation should require that the religious institution be designated "additionally insured" under the contractor's commercial general liability policy. This provision extends the contractor's liability protection to include the institution, so that the congregation may submit project-related liability claims to the contractor's insurance provider, rather than its own. The additionally insured language may be broadly inclusive; for example, designating "the religious entity and its directors, officers, clergy, employees, congregants, and volunteers."

The congregation's status as additionally insured should be noted in the contract. The congregation will then receive a certificate of insurance from the contractor's insurance company that explains the coverage available. Being a certificate holder also entitles the congregation to notification if there is a change or lapse in the policy. The congregation should not allow work to begin until it has the certificate in hand.

Congregations should consult their insurance agents to determine whether their own policy must be expanded to cover construction. Further, they should note that building consultants may also want to be named additionally insured under the contractor's insurance policy, although they should have their own professional liability insurance and commercial general liability insurance as well.

Licensing

The contractor's license number may appear in the contract; it should be verified. Contractor's licensing requirements vary from state to state. Congregations should check out the applicable regulations and make sure that their selected contractor is appropriately licensed. This information may often be found online.

Chapter 7.

Selecting a Bid

In Chapter 7 readers can learn to:

▶ Check that bidding requirements have been followed

▶ Compare prices comprehensively

▶ Consider experience, quality, and value when choosing a contractor

Regardless of whether a consultant is used, the process of bid evaluation demands high standards and strict attention. The congregation will aim to select a contractor whose knowledge and experience are well-documented, whose prices are fair, and whose attitude is friendly and open. Congregations should keep in mind that once a bid is signed by the religious institution it will become a contract: a legally binding agreement. All contract documents should be thoroughly read for completeness and accuracy before they are signed; if possible, the congregation should have legal counsel review them as well.

A consultant's involvement is valuable as bids are received; s/he will offer a professional opinion on the best one. A congregation working alone will need to use its resources to assess the bids received and negotiate the scope of work or price if necessary.

▶ Comparing and selecting with the help of a building consultant

The consultant will evaluate the bids received together with the congregation. S/he will want to make sure that the bid instructions have been followed and to discuss the bids in terms of pricing, alternates, and timing. The congregation should use these sessions to ask questions about anything that isn't clear; even if the consultant seems confident, the congregation's comfort and comprehension should take first priority. A decision shouldn't be made until the con-gregation is certain that it has selected the bid of the most qualified and fair contractor.

As the congregation works with the consultant, a price chart◉, similar to the one on the following page, may be helpful for comparing bids. If all of the contractor's bids are well over the congregation's budget, the consultant can help the congregation to reprioritize and reduce the scope of work. Alternatively, the consultant may choose to negotiate with contractors on the congregation's behalf.

Once a bid has been selected, the consultant will usually write up the AIA owner-contractor agreement. The congregation should review the AIA document before signing it and again check that all of its provisions are acceptable. Finally, the consultant should notify the contractors whose bids were not selected.

▶ Comparing and selecting without a building consultant

It has been recommended that congregations request a breakdown of lump sum costs. In order to analyze the bids received, the congregation will want to develop a chart like the one on the following page. It is based on the asphalt roof replacement described in Chapter 5.

ITEM	Contractor #1	Contractor #2	Contractor #3	Comments
Shingles				
Felt				
Sheathing				
Flashing				
Ice shield				
Drip edges				
Labor				

After receiving bids, the congregation would fill in each contractor's prices for the items listed. The completed chart would facilitate the congregation's process of comparison. It could make apparent, for example, that although Contractor #3's overall cost was greater, its prices for the felt and flashing were actually less expensive than that of Contractor #1 or #2.

Beyond price, the congregation may have to take into account quality; for example, one contractor might offer 15-pound felt and another 30-pound felt. The advice of contractors who are experienced but not bidding on the project, congregants who work with buildings, home improvement stores, and Web sites can be helpful for determining the value of higher quality items.

Congregations evaluating contractor's bids will also want to discuss their questions and demands with the contractors themselves. If one contractor's price is low but the materials are inferior or the job description is sparse, the congregation may request an estimate for higher quality materials or an addition to the scope of work. Congregations should remember that the lowest price is not necessarily the best bid; experience, quality, and value must all be considered.

Once a contractor is selected, the congregation should let the other contractors know that they did not receive the job. The congregation should then review the bid before signing it and make sure that all its provisions are clear and acceptable. If the congregation is uncertain about any part of it, advice should be sought from an uninterested party, such as a preservation organization or uninvolved contractor or architect. Again, when the bid is signed it becomes a legally binding contract. It is therefore imperative that materials, techniques, time periods, and costs be spelled out exactly. Clarifying ambiguities before signing is always easier than trying to do so after work has begun.

Chapter 8.

In Chapter 8 readers can learn to:

▶ Monitor the work and keep it on schedule

▶ Handle change orders

▶ Make progressive payments

▶ Understand substantial completion

▶ Prevent problems with well-planned communication

▶ Take steps towards conflict resolution

• **Payment requisition** Similar to an invoice, the contractor's written request for payment for work (or a portion of work) completed.

• **Change order** An amendment to the contract signed by the contractor and congregation (and building consultant, if applicable) verifying a change in conditions, timing, scope, or use of materials.

Implementation of the contract will need to be supervised by either the consultant or the congregation. Building consultants will generally oversee the contractor's work and review the contractor's payment requisitions. In the case of discrepancies, s/he will advise the congregation and communicate the problem to the contractor. If the congregation is working alone, it will need to supervise the work and communicate with the contractor about discrepancies and payments.

▶ When a building consultant supervises the contractor

Part of a building consultant's services usually includes "contract administration," referring to the signed agreement between the congregation and contractor. It basically means that s/he will make sure the contractor is fulfilling the intent of the plans and specifications. This can be done with a weekly survey during construction and a final assessment of the complete job. Some consultants additionally include close or frequent monitoring of the contractor's work. Congregations should review their consultant's intentions before work begins to avoid unmet expectations.

By taking on contract administration, the building consultant will also tend to logistic concerns. Details such as parking and utility usage will either be set in the contract or explained before work begins. The consultant will work with the contractor to develop a basic schedule, so that the project is executed in a timely matter. Finally, the consultant will tend to the more complicated matters of change orders, payment requisitions, and the final inspection.

Change orders

Because the contract is a legally binding document, changes to it must be made in writing. To illustrate: if the contractor is unable to order a material specified in the contract, another one can't simply be substituted—doing so would place the contractor in breach of contract. Instead, the consultant will issue a change order to be signed by all involved parties (the AIA's form is often used). The change order dictates that the specified adjustments are to be included as part of the original contract.

Making progressive payments

Most contracts employ progress payments: payment is not made all at once but at set times. The amount is determined by the percentage of work then completed. For example, the contract will specify a payment due on July 2. On that date, the contractor will assess how much work has been completed. If 35% of the total work is completed, the contractor will issue the congregation and consultant a payment requisition for 35% of the total contract sum. The building consultant is responsible for verifying that the portion has been completed; then the congregation issues payment.

• **Substantial completion** Point in a construction project when the work is basically finished, although clean up or details may require further attention.

• **Punch list** A list of items for the contractor to finish, developed by the owner and contractor (and building consultant, if one is involved) when the scope of work has almost been completed. May include site cleanup or painting of trim, for example.

In contracts providing for retainage, the retainage amount will be subtracted from progress payment requests. The retainage (usually 10% of the total cost) is not paid until the work has been accepted and the final payment made.

Completing the project

As the work draws to a close, the contractor will advise the consultant and the congregation that "substantial completion" has been reached. At that point, the work should basically be finished, even if details still require attention. The building consultant and a representative of the congregation, together with the contractor, will inspect the site and generate a "punch list" of final items for completion. After the punch list work has been done, the contractor will request that the final payment, including retainage, be made. The congregation or the consultant should perform a final survey before that payment is issued.

▶ When a congregation supervises the contractor

Before work is set to begin, the building committee must appoint one person to serve as the contractor's contact person, the liaison between contractor and congregation. The contact person will need to feel comfortable inspecting and discussing the contractor's work. If the contact person is unsure about a material or technique being used, s/he must ask the contractor for an explanation. Even if the contact person isn't a professional, the contractor should be willing to answer questions or discuss workmanship.

The contact person will also manage logistics, changes to the contract, payments, and project completion. To begin, the contact person should set up the site by designating an entrance and exit for the workers and defining what equipment and utilities the workers can use. These regulations should be written into the contract under "site provisions" before work begins. If they are not, the contact person must meet the contractor on the day work is set to begin and explain them.

The contact person will also be responsible for monitoring the work schedule. The contract should designate a start date and the number of days the job will take. If the congregation must cancel a day's work—for a funeral, for instance—the contact person should let the contractor know as soon as possible. If the contractor must amend the schedule, the contact person will want to request that the contractor put the change in writing and add it to the contract documents. Such a change might occur if the contractor has difficulty procuring a material and must delay the start date.

Changes and change orders

In general, changes to the contract should be made in writing, acknowledged by both parties,

Project publicity

Just as the owner of a house would be horrified to come home one day and find it unexpectedly under construction, congregants may be annoyed, put out, or highly irritated to discover contractors at work on their building. Unanticipated interference is always a nuisance; repair projects create their own specialized disturbances. As the date when contractors will begin work approaches, the building committee must publicize what will happen and when. Letting the building's regular users know what to expect will allow them to plan ahead and circumvent upsetting situations. The contractor's work schedule should be publicized with signs, announcements, or postings. More publicity ideas appear in Chapter 2. Even if the committee expects the construction to be a major inconvenience, its literature should focus on the beneficial end result as much as possible. The project will run far more smoothly if the congregation feels positively about the project.

and added to the contract documents. A change in the contract may be anything from substituting one material for another to increasing the amount of time the job will take; prices may be affected. If the contractor approaches the contact person about such a change, the contact person should request that a letter, or a more formal change order, be written and added to the contract documents. The AIA has a standard change order form that may be adapted. The contractor and a representative of the congregation should sign the change order before it takes effect.

Issuing a change order ensures that the contract remains consistent with the work done. Without an up-to-date contract, the congregation will have little recourse should something go wrong. Congregations working without building consultants must be especially careful to keep records of the construction work. Should a conflict arise, the congregation will want well-maintained records and thorough documentation to present to an arbitrator or judge.

Making payments

A small-scale project will usually have a fairly direct payment plan. Sometimes, the congregation will be required to make a deposit before the work is begun; in that case, another payment is often due when half the work is completed and the remaining balance is due upon completion. Other contractors may require no deposit but one or more periodic payments before the final balance is due.

For payments other than a deposit, the contact person should always feel confident about the work completed before the payment is issued. When the contractor has completed a designated portion of the job and is ready to be paid, an invoice or payment request will be issued to the congregation. For larger projects, an itemized list of materials expenses and labor is usually included. The contact person should inspect the work completed to verify that it has been done accurately. If a member of the congregation has had experience in design or construction, that person's assessment will be helpful. Any discrepancies should be addressed to the contractor for an explanation or correction. Once a satisfactory inspection has been made, the payment should be issued, minus the retainage (usually 10%) if applicable.

Completing the project

When the job is nearly complete (the contractor may advise the contact person that "substantial completion" has been reached), the contact person should make a thorough inspection of the site and point out items that have not yet been completed. For example, the site may not have been cleared of all materials, a tarp covering the entrance may need to be removed, or the contractor may still need a material to finish a cer-

Preventing problems

The contact person or building consultant should be the only individual who gives instructions to the contractor or makes changes to the contract. Often, there are lots of small repair jobs which need to be done around the building, and congregants may be tempted to request the contractor's assistance. But adding to the scope of work in this informal way is awkward and can cause the contractor to feel as if the congregation is taking advantage of its services. Further, it may delay the work on the actual contract.

tain task. These items will go on a "punch list." The contractor should not issue a final invoice until the punch list tasks have been completed. At that point, the contact person should survey the building once more before paying the contractor the amount due plus the accumulated retainage.

▶ Conflict resolution

Conflicts between the two parties signing a contract can come up unexpectedly. The congregation should always aim to discuss a discrepancy calmly and clearly with the contractor. Conflicts in the contract document require strict interpretation based on the plainest or most thoughtful language. For example, if there is a discrepancy about the scope of work or the number of units to be worked on, the specific wording is accepted over the general wording, and the typed or handwritten words prevail over the printed form. When numbers are expressed both in words and in numeric figures, the words are accepted.

In the event that a larger dispute occurs, over the subject of whether the contractor has fulfilled the scope of work, or whether all payments have been received, for instance, the contractor and a representative from the congregation—preferably someone with legal expertise—should first try to settle it themselves. If the dispute is not reconciled, mediation with a neutral, professional arbitrator is appropriate.

Proceeding in court is the third, final, most costly, and most time-consuming step. It should therefore be avoided if at all possible.

If a congregation working with a consultant has concerns about the contractor's work, it is best to communicate them to the consultant first. The consultant may have dealt with the problem or the contractor in the past and will be better equipped to develop a strategy for compromise. Congregations working alone should try to communicate their dissatisfaction to the contractor in a space that is comfortable for both parties.

Conclusion

In the Conclusion readers can continue to think about:

► Fundraising

► Maintenance

► Keeping records

Finally, there is no distinction to be made between the congregations working with or without a consultant. When the work is done, all project committees will thank their congregations and hold a tremendous party celebrating their ultimate success. (The proceeds from the event will go directly into a fund for future building repairs.) In fact, celebrations are important for public relations, as they call attention to a well-done job and thank the community for their patience during construction. Fundraising for future projects, maintenance, and record-keeping are also pertinent considerations once the project has drawn to a close.

Fundraising

Fundraising for the maintenance and preservation of the building should continue to be important to the congregational leadership, even after a major project has been completed. Although the committee may be reluctant to solicit donations at this point, it should at least generate a fundraising plan that takes into account repairs planned for the next five to ten years.

Maintenance

After the building has experienced a major improvement, the congregation will want to be vigilant about upkeep. In addition to making regular inspections and scheduling maintenance items annually, the congregation may want to consider developing a maintenance plan. A maintenance plan ◉ is a document that explains how the building should be cared for on a regular basis. A building consultant can be paid to generate a comprehensive one that describes each building element and lists appropriate techniques and materials for its upkeep. These usually contain some kind of calendar as well, which can be used to remind the congregation or its maintenance staff of all the items to do during each season. As an alternative, the congregation can develop its own maintenance plan based on a thorough building inspection and consultation with a custodian or other experienced individual. Such a maintenance plan might pay special attention to the building elements recently repaired.

Keeping records

In two years or five years or six months, when it's time for the committee to consider another repair project, it will want to begin by collecting information about previous repairs. As the committee completes each project, therefore, it should make sure that accurate, detailed records are kept: of people encountered, steps taken, caveats learned, and contracts signed. All of this information can be stored in a folder or file that will be readily accessible and understandable to the next generation of committee members.

The committee may want to consider using this book as an additional record. Copies of the bids it received can be paper-clipped to the chapters on bids, or the phone number of a particularly helpful organization can be written in the Introduction. Of course, by using this book as a recorded history, the committee assumes that future members will look to it as a resource. The Landmarks Conservancy hopes that this will be the case; that the book has been a helpful, relevant, and clear guide that will continue to serve congregations, like the buildings it discusses, for generations to come.

Appendix

Scenarios

Following are two scenarios for possible projects. In the first, the congregation is taking on a complex project with the help of a building consultant. In the second, the congregation is working alone to complete a basic repair. Each is expanded into a short case study in which the congregation goes through the steps described in the main text. Bold headings correspond to chapter titles, italicized text is a summary of the step taken, and plain text tells the narrative.

Readers must remember that these are fictional! Institutional needs vary and congregations may take paths different from those related here.

Scenario A

A complex project in which a building consultant is hired.

▶ Assessing the building

The congregation could identify several problems and needed to begin solving them.

The religious institution comprised a large congregation and a complex building. In the past, the congregation had made minor repairs to the structure, patching the roof or repairing the gutters as necessary. One summer, however, a leaking roof disrupted services. A subsequent inspection revealed that the stained glass windows were bowing and parts of the exterior masonry were crumbling. The congregation decided to take action.

▶ Assigning responsibility

The clergy, a congregational officer, and several other congregants formed a committee to begin planning repairs.

The congregation's officers met and voted to establish a project committee that would be responsible for planning and implementing repairs. The Vice President, Robert, volunteered to be the project committee chairperson. He asked other interested congregants to join. The clergy also agreed to participate in the committee. At the first committee meeting, Robert shared a packet of information he'd received from a preservation organization. An immediate goal was set: to find out about making a long-term repair plan.

▶ Working with consultants

After consulting with a preservation organization, the committee decided to hire a preservation architect to perform a conditions survey.

Robert called the preservation organization for advice, explaining that he'd read about a conditions survey and wanted to know more. The project committee wanted to identify the building's largest threats and come up with a plan to solve them. The organization's staff person said that hiring a preservation architect to perform a survey certainly seemed like the right thing to do. The survey would help the congregation understand the deterioration and prioritize repair projects. It would also provide cost estimates, which would help with budgeting and fundraising.

Robert's committee met to evaluate the congregation's finances. By planning a fundraising campaign, the committee decided it could afford to undertake and implement a survey. Robert solicited proposals from three architects recommended by the preservation organization. One architect had extensive preservation experience and several references from other religious institutions. Her fee was within the congregation's budget and the committee felt comfortable talking to her. After Robert received positive comments from her references, the building committee decided to hire her.

▶ Planning the work

The architect performed a conditions survey. She helped the congregation to identify three repairs to be completed in a first phase of work.

The architect surveyed the building over several weeks before writing up her findings and recommendations. She presented the survey to the entire congregation, using a slide show to illustrate the $1 million worth of repairs that would ultimately be needed: from replacing the slate roof to evaluating the stained glass to cleaning the masonry facade. She assured the congregation that, taken step by step, the repairs could be completed successfully over a ten year period.

The architect worked with the building committee to develop an affordable first phase of work. It included three projects: replacing the slate roof over the sanctuary, repointing the masonry in that area, and doing a sample cleaning near the exterior entrance. The roof work and repointing were priorities because they would make the building watertight. Although the cleaning wasn't a technical priority, the architect and committee agreed that it would be visibly impressive to the congregation in a way the other repairs might not be. Over the next six months, the committee raised just enough money to cover the phase and then let the architect know it was ready to go on.

▶ Soliciting contractors' bids

The architect was hired to develop contract documents and supervise construction for the first phase of work. She wrote plans and specifications to send out with contractors' bid packages.

The architect prepared an owner-architect agreement, or contract, under which she would develop contract documents and administer the construction. Once the congregation had signed the agreement, she generated plans and specifications to describe the exact way that each repair should take place. Then she compiled the information in a bid package, which she sent to three qualified contractors.

▶ Selecting a bid

An experienced contractor was selected who had expertise in one area and would hire subcontractors to complete the other parts of the job.

The architect and the building committee reviewed the contractors' proposals. The architect recommended one general contractor with whom she had worked before. He had proposed to do the roof work with his in-house team and hire a masonry specialist for the repointing and cleaning. On other projects, the architect had found the mason's work to be satisfactory. The committee reviewed the congregation's budget and estimated that they could afford the recommendation. The architect notified the contractor and developed an American Institute of Architects (AIA) owner-contractor agreement

to serve as the contract. A start date was set and the contract was signed.

▶ Supervising the contractor's work

The architect periodically assessed the contractor's work and made inspections before payments were issued. At one point, she found that the craftsmanship deviated from her specifications. The architect notified the contractor and had the work corrected. As the project neared completion, the architect developed a punch list of tasks to be finished before the final payment would be made.

The general contractor had proposed to complete the job within twelve weeks. First, his team would replace the slate roof; then the masons would repoint and clean the designated areas. The architect was informed of the contractor's schedule and visited the site twice each week to monitor the work. During one of her visits, she noticed that the slate installation was not being done precisely as she had specified. She immediately pointed the problem out to the contractor, who reviewed the specifications with her and corrected the work.

The contract set a payment date for four weeks after work began. At that time, the contractor assessed that he had completed 35% of the project. He sent the consultant and congregation a payment requisition for 35% of the total cost of the project, less the agreed-upon 10% retainage. The consultant performed an inspection of the work completed and confirmed that 35% had been finished and done well. She advised the congregation to issue the requested payment.

As the project neared completion and the final payment date, Robert reviewed the work with the architect and developed a punch list of work still to be done. The congregation issued its final payment, including the retainage, once those items had been finished.

Scenario B

A simple project completed without a building consultant

▶ Assessing the building

The congregation had an active leak in the sanctuary and the office. After months of patching the asphalt shingles, the congregation could see that a new roof was needed.

The religious institution belonged to a small community. Its general operating budget was usually tight, and building maintenance had never been a priority. For months, the congregation had been aware of a leak in the sanctuary and the office. A custodian had inspected the asphalt roof and found a number of deteriorated areas, which he patched with tar. After a few months, however, the leaks recurred. The congregation decided it was time to replace the roof.

▶ Assigning responsibility

Three congregants volunteered to serve on the project committee. One member would be the contact person.

At the congregation's monthly leadership meeting, one congregant volunteered to develop a project committee to replace the roof. Although she had no previous experience, she had always valued the building's history and wanted to preserve it. She asked two other congregants to serve on her committee, one of whom, Evelyn, volunteered to be the contact person for planning and construction.

▶ Working with consultants

The committee decided not to hire an outside consultant, but to seek bids from specialized roofing contractors.

The congregation assessed its finances and allocated $15,000 from an emergency reserve fund to the project. Evelyn called a local preservation organization for advice on where to begin. The staff person said that she always recommended hiring an architect for an overall evaluation. Still, she knew that the architect's fees would account for a significant portion of the reserves; if the congregation didn't have major fundraising plans but had identified a specific scope of work, the money might be better spent on a specialized roofing contractor.

Evelyn presented the organization's advice to the building committee. The committee members' main goal was to do the work before the leak caused major damage. They considered the small size of the roof, the fact that the roof (and its repair) were fundamental to the structure's overall longevity, and their limited short-term fundraising prospects. They decided not to hire an architect but to seek bids directly from experienced roofing contractors.

▶ Planning the work

After doing some research, the committee decided how to replace the roof.

The building committee wanted to understand exactly what needed to be done before approaching contractors. Evelyn decided to meet with the custodian to examine the roof. They found a layer of asphalt roofing beneath the top one, and some single shingles that the custodian identified as cedar. Another committee member did some research and found that the top layer of roofing was architectural shingle that had exceeded its life span; originally, the roof had been covered with cedar shingles.

Evelyn went to a home improvement store to ask about how the roof could be replaced. The sales manager said that cedar would be beyond the congregation's budget. He recommended tearing off the old roofing and installing 40-year architectural shingles that would resemble the historic cedar. He explained that new flashing would really waterproof the building and suggested 20-ounce copper; he also thought that the sheathing should be replaced, as necessary. The committee decided to approach contractors for bids based on his advice.

▶ Soliciting contractors' bids

The committee gave a scope of work and bidding requirements to three recommended contractors. Evelyn contacted the preservation organization for referrals of roofing contractors with preservation experience. She called three contractors, arranging a site visit with each.

During the visits, Evelyn gave the contractors bidding requirements. The committee had used the sales manager's technical language to describe the job and requested that each bid include a list of material costs as well as a total price. It also asked that proof of insurance, available start date, and relevant warranty information be included in all bids.

▶ Selecting a bid

The committee consulted an adviser and decided upon the proposal that offered the most comprehensive waterproofing package. It elected to begin a fundraising campaign to cover the extra expense.

Evelyn received the contractor's bids. She made up a chart that listed their total costs and the prices for each material. The third contractor had included an ice shield and drip edges, which the others had not; that bid's total cost was

higher. Still, its prices for the other materials were lower than those of the first two.

Evelyn called a member of the congregation who worked for a general contracting firm and asked for his advice. He believed that the ice shield and drip edges were worth the extra expense because they would protect the roof and masonry in the event of heavy rain or snow. The building committee wanted to select the most comprehensive proposal but knew the congregation did not have enough money in its budget. They decided to hold a fundraising event to cover the extra expense. One month later, the money was raised and the contractor hired.

▶ Supervising the contractor's work

After paying the contractor his deposit, work began. One building committee member made regular site visits to the site. She checked that the contractor was working consistently and that the congregation was functioning adequately. She assessed the contractor's work before making payments.

Two weeks before the work was scheduled to begin, Evelyn met the team at the building to show them the site and give the contractor a deposit of half the cost of the job. She visited every other day while work was in process to assess that it was not disrupting the congregation unnecessarily.

The contractor let Evelyn know when the

work was nearly completed. Then she toured the site with the contractor and the congregant with contracting experience. They inspected the work and developed a punch list of unfinished items. When the punch list was completed, Evelyn had the congregation issue its final payment for the remainder of the job.

Sample Documents

These are roughly based on Scenarios A and B.

Chapter 3. Working with consultants

- *Prequalification questions for interviewing potential consultants or contractors*
- *Request for proposals for a conditions survey*

Chapter 4. Planning the Work

- *Conditions survey excerpt, showing recommended repairs*

Chapter 5. Soliciting Contractors' Bids

- *Simple bid package*
- *Qualification form*

Chapter 6. Understanding the Contract

- *Simple contract*

Chapter 7. Selecting a Bid

- *Price comparison chart*

Conclusion

- *Maintenance plan excerpt, with recommendations for one repaired element*

prequalification questions

from Chapter 3

The following questions are intended for preliminary screening of potential consultants or contractors. They can help to narrow a general list to those that are able to meet the congregation's basic requirements. Such candidates should then be sent requests for proposals or bid packages, which may demand further qualifications as presented on page 54.

Prequalification of consultants:

What is your background in historic preservation?

Have you ever worked with a religious institution?
What were the greatest challenges involved?

How would you approach project planning?
What is included in your typical conditions survey contract?
How often would you expect to meet with the building committee?

Would you be able to offer advice about phasing and fundraising?

Would you be able to make a presentation to the entire congregation once the survey is completed?

How do you envision your role once a project has been established, especially in terms of contract administration and working with the contractor?

How many years have you practiced?
Are you licensed by the state?
What insurance do you carry?

Prequalification of contractors:

Do you have any background in historic preservation?
(also: in the specific type of project proposed, e.g. roofwork)

Have you ever worked with a religious institution?
What were the greatest challenges involved?

Approximately how long would it take you to complete the job?
When could you begin?

How many years have you been in business?
Are you licensed by the county or state?
What insurance do you carry?

request for proposals

from Chapter 3

This is a request for proposals that would be given to prequalified consultants. Then they would tour the site and generate a proposal for completing the conditions survey described. The request for proposals is different from a bid package in that it asks the consultant to develop an appropriate methodology for executing the work, not to bid on a set job. Proposals must therefore be compared thoughtfully; congregations should consider the approach of the consultants as well as their prices.

Request for Proposals, March 31, 2003

The Congregation of Millsville is seeking the services of a preservation architect to conduct an existing conditions survey of its building complex located at 90 North Street, Millsville.

Services required:
1. *Exterior Building Survey:* Assess and analyze the existing conditions of the envelope of the building complex.
2. *Structural Engineering Survey:* Investigate the condition of existing structural systems, including foundation, walls and roof.
3. *Mechanical Engineering Survey:* Investigate the condition of the plumbing, electrical, HVAC (heating, ventilation, and air conditioning) systems, and smoke detection and fire suppression systems.
4. *Report:* Based on the surveys, develop a written and illustrated report including prioritized recommendations and cost estimates for repair or restoration of deteriorated elements and systems.

At this time, the scope of work specifically does not include: a separate stained glass window survey, the preparation of drawings or construction documents (including plans and specifications), and project management. Copies of original construction drawings are available for use by the architect.

The existing conditions report should include the following components:
1. Brief history of construction and maintenance
2. Description of existing conditions in clear, non-technical language, including any reports by engineers or other specialists and probable causes of any noted failures or deterioration
3. Annotated photographs
4. List or spreadsheet organizing recommended items according to urgency, with cost estimates

Upon completion of the above, the consultant shall submit two copies of the report. The consultant shall present the findings and recommendations at two meetings with congregational leadership and members, each not to exceed two hours.

Preservation Status and Minimum Qualifications:
The building complex is listed on the State and National Registers of Historic Places. Past experience with historic preservation projects and, in particular, religious properties, is essential for the successful completion of this project. All work carried out must comply with the Secretary of the Interior's Standards for the Treatment of Historic Properties.

Submission of Proposals:
Proposals should include a project description, brief narrative statement of approach, and the estimated time schedule for completion; plus, proposed cost of the exterior, structural, and mechanical surveys, an allowance estimate for anticipated expenses not detailed above and for reimbursable expenses, and a total for the entire scope of work. Staffing structure and hourly billing rates of the architectural firm should also be included.

Applicants should submit contact information for similar projects completed recently, and a copy of the survey produced, if available. Resumes for staff members, describing qualifications and experience relevant to the project, are requested as well.

Proposals may be sent to the attention of Mr. Robert Smith, Congregation of Millsville at 90 North Street, Millsville, (555) 555-8100. He will be contacting you next week to discuss the proposed scope of work and schedule a site visit.

conditions survey

from Chapter 4

This is an excerpt from a conditions survey. A full survey would include the consultant's findings and recommendations for repair. The portion here shows only the recommendations, divided into three categories: Prioirities/Major Repairs, Maintenance Projects, and Overall Maintenance. The congregation and the architect would work together to come up with a phased plan for executing the projects described.

Conditions Survey

Based on a through assessment, our office recommends that the following repairs be undertaken. Major Repair items have been designated by urgency: Immediate Concern, Near Future (to be done within five years), or Long Range (to be done within 15 years).

Priorities: Major Repairs

Most of the following can be phased, to be completed over the course of five to ten years. As the sanctuary is the oldest part of the building complex, however, the roof replacement there should be undertaken as soon as possible. It is recommended that the repointing take place shortly afterwards.

1. **Immediate Concern:** *Sanctuary roof replacement*

- Removal of all slates
- Replacement of slates and flashing
- Relining and reconnection of gutters
- Removal of all flashing
- Installation of ice barrier and snow guard

Estimated cost: $250,000

2. **Near Future:** *Sanctuary repointing*

- Removal of all deteriorated mortar on four sides of sanctuary
- Replacement of mortar with appropriate mixture

Estimated cost: $100,000

3. **Near Future:** *Slate roof repair for remainder of building*

- Removal of first five rows of slate around perimeter, as well as at corners and specified deteriorated areas
- Removal of all flashing
- Replacement of slates and flashing
- Removal of all tar around roof
- Installation of ice barrier and snow guards

Estimated cost: $75,000

4. **Long Range:** *Stained glass window repair*

- Evaluation of stained glass windows by qualified conservator
- Releading and replacement of glass as necessary
- Reinstallation of windows in secured window frames, with support system elements replaced as necessary.

Estimated cost: $100,000

Routine Maintenance Plan

These projects don't require significant fundraising and should be done as noted. They may also be combined with more major repairs in work phases.

1. Clean gutters and downspouts regularly, especially once they have been replaced on the sanctuary *(Perform every 3 months)*
2. Designate all exits with clearly labeled signs *(As soon as possible)*
3. Replace locks on front and rear doors *(As soon as possible)*
4. Clean classroom windows regularly *(Perform every 3-6 months)*

Overall Maintenance

It is recommend that a maintenance plan be developed and implemented. This will help ensure that repaired elements are cared for well and that fewer major repairs are required in the future. In addition to outlining protection of the building envelope against water infiltration, it should explain how to maintain repaired elements.

simple bid package

from Chapter 5

This is a simple bid package that a congregation working without a consult-ant would send to prequalified contractors. The project scope is of utmost importance. It must be very specific, derived from careful research and consultation with preservation professionals, experienced contractors, and/or product manufactur-ers. The other components warrant attention as well, since many contractors will not include their references or an assurance on historic preservation unless requested to do so.

The Millsville Congregation

12 Main Street, Millsville, New York

1. **Project scope:**
- *Remove all asphalt shingles, felt, and flashing; also, all deteriorated sheathing.*
- *Install 40-year architectural asphalt shingles.*
- *Install a single layer of 30-lb. asphalt-saturated felt.*
- *Install 20-oz. copper flashing in all valleys.*
- *Replace deteriorated sheathing with new, to match existing, as necessary.*
- *Install new ice shield to prevent snow and ice accumulation.*

2. *Bid submission:* All bids should be sent to Ms. Evelyn Wright, Roof Committee, at the above address by March 1, 2003. Tours of the site may be arranged by calling the congregation's main office at 555-1212. Bids must include expected start date and duration, plus acknowledgement of the specifications following.

3. *Pricing:* Please provide a lump sum figure for roof cover replacement and flashing replacement and break down materi-als costs in the space provided below. Progress payments are preferred and retainage of 10% required.

4. *Insurance:* Comprehensive General Liability is required, as are workers' compensation and automobile liability insur-ance. The congregation is expected to be listed Additionally Insured under the contractor's policy and receive all relevant certificates before work commences.

5. *Qualifications:* Please include contacts for at least three historic buildings on which you have recently worked; houses of worship are preferred.

6. *Historic Preservation:* This building has been designated historic on the State and National Registers of Historic Places. All work completed should be consistent with the Secretary of the Interior's Standards for the Treatment of Historic Properties.

7. *Scheduling:* Contractor will cancel work for a 24-hour period if given 12 hours notice in the event the premises must be used for unanticipated services (e.g., a funeral).

8. *Site provisions:* The contractor must maintain a clean site. The contractor must provide industrial dumpsters as neces-sary. Access to restrooms and outdoor hoses will be provided. Use of all utilities must be verified, before construction begins, at the congregation's office.

9. *Materials and workmanship warranties:* Copies should be attached to bid as available.

Pricing

Total cost for replacement of asphalt shingles and flashing: $_____

Unit prices:		*Unit cost for replacement of sheathing:*	
Shingles (per square, 10′ x 10′)	$_____	Materials (per square foot)	$_____
Felt (per square foot)	$_____	Labor (per hour)	$_____
Flashing (per linear foot)	$_____		
Ice shield (per linear foot)	$_____		
Labor (per hour)	$_____		

qualification form

from Chapter 5

This form may be included in a request for proposals or bid package. When it is returned, congregations should make sure nothing unsound is revealed. The congregation should call the contacts listed for a review of the consultant's or contractor's skill, thoroughness, attitude, professionalism, and friendliness.

1. General qualifications

Please record the following information about the firm and its history.

Firm name: _____

Address: _____

_____

Contact person: _____

Phone number: _____

Signature: _____

Other names under which the business has operated:

_____

Type of business *(corporation or partnership)*:

_____

Date of formation: _____

Principal location: _____

Names of officers or partners: _____

Insurance policies and levels: _____

Has the firm ever defaulted on a contract or had work terminated for non-performance? If so, describe the project, listing the owner, date, and circumstances.

_____

_____

_____

_____

_____

_____

_____

_____

2. Experience qualifications

Please list projects involving historic buildings with similar scopes of work to the one described, preferably completed with in the past 5 years.
These should have been done in compliance with the Secretary of the Interior's Standards for the Treatment of Historic Properties.

Project #1

Property: _____ Original date of construction: _____

Scope of work: _____

Completion date: _____ Cost: $ _____

Owner/Contact: _____ Phone number: _____

Architect: _____

Project #2

Property: _____ Original date of construction: _____

Scope of work: _____

Completion date: _____ Cost: $ _____

Owner/Contact: _____ Phone number: _____

Architect: _____

Project #3

Property: _____ Original date of construction: _____

Scope of work: _____

Completion date: _____ Cost: $ _____

Owner/Contact: _____ Phone number: _____

Architect: _____

simple contract

from Chapter 6

This is a contract that may be received in response to the bid package on page 53. For small jobs, contracting companies usually use simple form proposals that are signed and become contracts. In general, additional provisions (such as those on page 56) will be included only if requested by the congregation in the bid package.

continued on page 56

A-1 Roofing Company
4 South Street
Millsville, New York
555-8989

February 28, 2003

Ms. Evelyn Wright, *Roof Committee*
The Millsville Congregation
12 Main Street
Millsville, New York
555-1212

CONTRACT

Scope of work:

1. Remove all asphalt shingles, felt, flashing; also, all deteriorated sheathing.
2. Install 40-year architectural asphalt shingles. *Brand:* AllDry. *Color:* Medium Cedar.
3. Install a single layer of 30-lb. asphalt-saturated felt. Apply horizontally.
4. Install 20-oz. copper flashing in all valleys.
5. Replace deteriorated sheathing with new, to match existing, as necessary.
6. Install ice shield at a minimum of three feet above intersections where eaves meet a wall, centered on all valleys, and around all penetrations. Also 8 inches up where walls intersect roof.

Price: $_____ *(See breakdown and additional costs for sheathing attached.)*
This bid is good for sixty days after issuance.

Work to commence: March 15, 2003. *Expected duration:* 12 weeks.

Payment Schedule

$_____ deposit due upon signing (25% minus 10% retainage)
$_____ due April 26, 2003 (50% minus 10% retainage)
$_____ due at substantial completion (25% minus 10% retainage)
$_____ 10% retainage due at completion of punch list

simple contract (continued)

continued from page 55

Additional Provisions

1. *Site:* The contractor will maintain a clean site and be responsible for debris removal. Use of all utilities will be verified before construction begins.
2. *Scheduling:* 12-hour notice must be given for interruptions in work due to special circumstances.
3. *Warranties:* Work is warrantied for five years for defects in construction. Manufacturer's warranty is attached.
4. Historic nature of building is understood and will be protected to the best of our ability.

A-1 Roofing Company holds Comprehensive General Liability, workers' compensation, and automobile liability insurance. The congregation will be listed Additionally Insured and furnished with proof of insurance before work begins.

Signed

_____   _____

The Millsville Congregation   A-1 Roofing Company
                                                    NY State License no._____

Date:_____   Date:_____

References:
Jane Plum, Springfield Congregation, Springfield. 555-2000.
Ross Lee, 55 Old Bridge Street, Springfield. 555-3111.
Amanda Rebb, 90 North Avenue, Millsville. 555-8888.

Pricing Sheet

Total cost for replacement of asphalt shingles, felt, and flashing: $_____

Unit prices:

Shingles (per square)	$_____
Felt (per square foot)	$_____
Flashing (per linear foot)	$_____
Ice shield (per linear foot)	$_____
Labor (per hour)	$_____

Unit cost for replacement of sheathing:

Materials (per square foot)	$_____
Labor (per hour)	$_____

price comparison chart

from Chapter 7

An architect working with a congregation may prepare a chart like this one to analyze the bids received from contractors. Based on the technical specifications enumerated in the bid package, it provides space to compare the contractors' costs for each task or material, as well as their total prices. It also helps to understand whether contractors have assessed the job appropriately; if two contractors anticipate that 200 square feet of roofing is necessary and a third 700, it is likely that the third contractor has estimated poorly. The architect should fill in and review the chart carefully and then interpret the data for the congregation.

continued on page 58

Congregation of Millsville
90 North Street
Tower Restoration Project

Construction		ACME Contracting		USA Restoration, Inc.		Ajax Construction Corp.	
Work Item *(materials and labor)*	*Unit of measurement*	*# Units (anticipated)*	*Total Cost*	*# Units (anticipated)*	*Total Cost*	*# Units (anticipated)*	*Total Cost*
1. Remove existing roofing, flashing, and tiles	*square foot*						
2. Scrape and paint all roof framing steel	*linear foot*						
3. Remove and re-anchor roof ornament	*anchor*						
4. Install new wood sheathing	*square foot*						
5. Install new copper roofing	*square foot*						
6. Install new copper troughs	*square foot*						
7. Construct copper crickets	*square foot*						
8. Install copper base flashing	*linear foot*						
9. Provide ice and snow guards	*linear foot*						
10. Install copper ridge caps	*linear foot*						
11. Install new diverters	*diverter*						
12. Install new bronze drain heads	*drain head*						
13. Install new roof hatch	*hatch*						
14. Rake and repoint brownstone	*linear foot*						
15. Rake and repoint brick	*square foot*						
Section Totals		$		$		$	

price comparison (continued)

continued from page 57

Congregation of Millsville
90 North Street
Tower Restoration Project

General Catagories	ACME Contracting	USA Restoration, Inc.	Ajax Construction Corp.
	Cost	Cost	Cost
1. Temporary shoring and hoisting			
2. Provide and maintain exterior scaffolding			
3. Perform all demolition and clean-up			
4. Provide all testing and special reviews			
5. Provide all samples and product literature			
6. Provide and maintain all permits			
7. Provide new lightning protection			
Section Totals	$	$	$

Other Items	ACME Contracting	USA Restoration, Inc.	Ajax Construction Corp.
	Cost	Cost	Cost
1. General conditions			
2. Contract performance bond			
3. Overhead and profit			
4. Temporary electrical supply			
5. Temporary plumbing supply			
Section Totals	$	$	$
Overall Totals	$	$	$

maintenance plan

from the Conclusion

Once a project is completed, the congregation may want to have its consultant develop a maintenance plan. The plan will explain how the congregation can care for its building on an ongoing basis. Often, the plan is divided by building element and includes an annual task calendar or checklist. Here is a sample page that details care for ornamental metalwork.

Maintenance Plan

Element: Ornamental Metalwork.
A new handrail was designed and installed in March 2002. Supplemental banner posts were installed the following year.

Contractor: Finest Metalworks
1500 North Avenue
Springfield, New York
800-555-9999.

Cyclical Maintenance

Long term: Upon any signs of rust or corrosion, all surfaces should be properly prepared and re-coated as follows: *Carefully remove all rust, dust, oil, grease, and moisture. Select a complete paint system of primers and finish coats from a single major paint manufacturer and follow its written instructions for application to ferrous metal. Two primer coats are recommended.*

Inspect annually for: Broken welds. *To repair: weld loose connections. Do not epoxy.*

Loose connections at footings. *To repair: regrout.*

Rust and impact damage. *To repair: properly prepare and paint any exposed metal (see instructions under Long term maintenance, above).*

Coating: Touch-up every 3-5 years.
Recoat every 8-12 years.

Materials: Handrail: Iron
Life expectancy: 75-100 years.

Bibliography:

Ornamental Metal, SpecGUIDE G05700.
Construction Specifications Institute, 1989.
Weaver, Martin E. "Chapter 9: Architectural Metalwork," *Conserving Buildings: A Guide to Techniques and Materials.*
  New York: John Wiley & Sons, Inc., 1993.

Prepared November 2003.

This document has been adapted from a maintenance plan prepared and copyrighted by Walter Sedovic Architects of Irvington-on-Hudson, New York, for the Mamaroneck United Methodist Church.

Glossary

American Institute of Architects (AIA) A professional association of accredited architects, with chapters throughout the country. The AIA has several fill-in documents, such as the Owner-Architect Agreement and the Owner-Contractor Agreement, that are frequently used by architects working with congregations.

Arbitration Resolving a dispute using a neutral party rather than a court proceeding.

Architect Someone who designs buildings; a preservation architect analyzes existing building conditions and plans and oversees the administration of restoration projects. Legally, the term applies to professionals licensed by a state to practice architecture.

Asphalt Roofing A roofing material made with asphalt, available in rolls or shingles.

As-built Drawings Architectural drawings completed after the construction of a building; these may vary considerably from the original plans.

Bid An offer submitted by a contractor to complete a scope of work for a named price. When submitted in response to a bid package, other materials or information requested should be provided with the bid.

Bid Package A set of documents, developed by a congregation or building consultant, used to solicit contractors' bids. These should explain the congregation's expectations for the project as well as the form in which bids should be submitted. In addition to describing the scope of work with a written statement, or with plans and specifications, they may include: pricing forms, instructions to bidders, qualification forms, non-collusion affidavits, and other addenda.

Bidding Period As defined in the bid package, the time given to contractors to evaluate the package and submit a bid.

Bond Also called surety bond. Legal document arranging for a surety company to financially compensate the congregation in case the contractor defaults. The contractor must pay the surety company for this coverage; the cost is usually passed on to the congregation.

Building Envelope The primary exterior planes enclosing a building that protect it from water infiltration, including the exterior walls, roof, foundation, windows, and doors.

Certificate for Payment A written statement, from the building consultant to the owner, confirming the amount of money due to the contractor for work completed. Issued following the contractor's payment requisition and the consultant's subsequent inspection.

Certificate of Insurance A document issued by an insurance company to the congregation, stating the types, amounts, and effective dates of the contractor's insurance. Used for proof of insurance; the contractor may request one from the congregation's insurance company as well.

Change Order An amendment to the contract signed by the contractor and congregation (and building consultant, if applicable) verifying a change in conditions, timing, scope, or use of materials.

Conditions Survey A comprehensive, holistic evaluation of a building, prepared by a preservation consultant, that identifies its features and materials as well as its deficiencies and their causes. Generally based on visual inspection but can include physical probes if necessary. The survey report includes recommendations for repair projects, prioritized by urgency, and, usually, cost estimates for the work.

Construction Documents A term for the combined plans and specifications, which are generated by the building consultant and included in the contract to instruct the contractor how to execute the project.

Construction Management Professional project management services including cost estimation, scheduling, and contract administration, performed for the congregation by a specially trained individual or firm. A construction manager is usually hired in addition to the building consultant for substantial projects.

Contract A legally enforceable agreement (sometimes referred to as "the agreement") between the congregation and the building consultant, or the congregation and contractor, or the congregation, building consultant, and contractor.

Contract Administration The part of an architect or other building consultant's services that includes overseeing the execution of the contract between the owner and contractor. Depending on the consultant, this may consist of frequent monitoring of the contractor's work, project management, or periodic visits to the site.

Contract Documents The documents included or referred to in the contract; includes the signed agreement and construction documents, change orders, and pricing or qualification forms as applicable.

Contract Sum Price stated in the contract as the total amount owed by the congregation to the contractor. May be paid progressively if allowed in the contract and may be adjusted with a change order.

Contractor One who undertakes responsibility for the performance of construction work.

Drawings See Plans.

Drip Edge A strip which extends beyond other parts of a roof to direct rainwater off of it.

Engineer Licensed professional who practices engineering. Many specializations exist; structural and mechanical engineers are those most commonly hired for building preservation and construction projects.

Errors and Omissions Insurance Professional liability insurance that protects a consultant from mistakes arising from negligence or miscalculation.

Flashing A thin waterproof material placed to prevent water penetration and/or provide drainage, especially at roof corners, between a roof and wall, and over exterior door openings and windows.

General Contractor A contractor whose firm performs, or assembles subcontractors to perform, all types of contracting tasks including interior, exterior, and systems work.

Gutter A shallow channel of metal or wood set immediately below and along the roof or eaves of a building to carry rainwater away from the roof.

Historic Structure Report An evaluation of a building based on a conditions survey but also including historical research and analysis. Using historical records and images, the preservation consultant generates a report of how the building has been altered over time. Because it is so comprehensive, it is usually performed only in anticipation of a major restoration, not to plan basic repairs or maintenance.

Lump Sum Agreement A contract in which a specific amount is set forth as the total payment for the contractor. This payment may be made progressively or broken down by unit pricing.

Maintenance Plan A calendar, schedule, or list of procedures intended to manage and direct regular upkeep of a building.

Master Plan A document or set of plans proposing a change in the design or use of a building; may be undertaken by congregations wanting to enlarge their building or reconfigure its use of space.

Mortar A mixture usually containing sand, lime, and cement, which is mixed with water and applied with a trowel to a surface (See Pointing), where it becomes hard in place. Commonly used to bond the spaces between brick, stone, or cement block.

National Register of Historic Places The official US list of cultural resources worthy of preservation. Authorized under the National Historic Preservation Act of 1966, it primarily aims to identify, evaluate, and protect historic sites, rather than to regulate them. Nominations for sites, buildings, objects, or districts are made through the State Historic Preservation Office for the National Parks Service.

Non-collusion Affidavit A notarized statement by a contractor that an accompanying bid has been prepared without collusion with other contractors.

Owner-Architect Agreement A contract between the architect and congregation for professional services. The American Institute of Architects (AIA) form is commonly used.

Owner-Contractor Agreement A contract between the owner and the contractor for a construction project. If an architect is involved, s/he often prepares, reviews, and signs the document as well; an AIA form is commonly used.

Payment Requisition Similar to an invoice, the contractor's written request for payment for work (or a portion of work) completed.

Permit Authorization from a municipal agency allowing a specific construction project. One or more permits, issued by agencies such as the Buildings Department or the Landmarks Commission, may be necessary for repair work, depending on local laws and the building's landmark status; congregations should find out before signing a contract to execute work.

Plans Also called Drawings. Documents generated by an architect or other building consultant to graphically describe the project to the contractor. Almost always accompanied and explained by written technical specifications. Together, the plans and specifications form the construction documents of the bid package or contract.

Pointing The application, with a trowel, of mortar in between brick or masonry joints; "repointing" refers to removing deteriorated mortar and reapplying a mortar mixture.

Prequalification The process of investigating the qualifications of prospective consultants or contractors *before* proposals or bids are solicited.

Preservation Saving old and historic sites, buildings, and objects from destruction or deterioration by working for their continued use. According to the Secretary of the Interior's Standards, "the act or process of applying measures to sustain the existing form, integrity, and material of a building or structure, and the existing form and vegetative cover of a site. . . may include stabilization work, where necessary, as well as ongoing maintenance of the historic building materials."

Preservation Commission Often, as in New York City, called a Landmarks Preservation Commission. A local or county board that designates landmarks and regulates significant changes to landmarked districts and buildings.

Professional Liability Insurance Insurance designed to insure an architect or engineer against claims for damages resulting from professional negligence.

Progress Payment A partial payment of a lump sum, based on the portion of the work completed. The contract must specify if and how progress payments are to be employed.

Proposal Although proposal and bid are often used interchangeably, a proposal is usually a response to an open-ended work scope (fix the leaking roof, for example), while a bid is an offer made for a defined scope (replace the roof cover with 40-year asphalt shingle). A proposal is most often requested from consultants but may also be useful for understanding how different contractors would approach the same problems.

Punch List A list of items for the contractor to finish, developed by the owner and contractor (and building consultant, if one is involved) when the scope of work has almost been completed. May include site cleanup or painting of trim, for example.

Reconstruction A term employed in the Secretary of the Interior's Standards to describe the act of reproducing by new construction the exact form and detail of a vanished building, structure, or object, or a part thereof, as it appeared at a specific period of time.

Rehabilitation A term employed in the Secretary of the Interior's Standards to describe the act of repairing a property for an efficient contemporary use while preserving its history, architecture, and culture.

Renovation Modernization of old buildings, often without an interest in preservation.

Repointing See Pointing.

Request for Proposals A document describing work, usually a conditions survey, that a congregation wants done by a building consultant. In turn, the consultant will submit a proposed method and price for completing the job. The request for proposals is different from a bid package (given to contractors) in that the consultant is expected to help develop the job, not just bid on a defined task.

Restoration A term employed in the Secretary of the Interior's Standards to describe the act of recovering the form and details of a property and its setting as it appeared at a particular period, through removal of later materials or replacement of deteriorated ones.

Retainage A portion (usually 10%) withheld from progress payments to the contractor until the job has been completely accepted by the owner (and building consultant if applicable). The accumulated retainage is paid with the last and final payment.

Scope of Work A description of the project to be executed.

Section 106 Provision in the National Historic Preservation Act of 1966 aimed at ensuring that historic properties are given due consideration in the planning of federal projects or actions. A Section 106 Review must be undertaken to determine whether federally funded projects will have an adverse effect on properties listed on or eligible for listing on the State and National Register of Historic Places.

Section 14.09 Provision in the New York State Parks, Recreation, and Historic Preservation Law of 1980 with the same aim as Section 106 (above), regarding the planning of state funded projects or actions.

Sheathing Material applied over building rafters to serve as a base for a roof or wall covering.

Specifications Written by the architect (or other building consultant) to explain the exact technical requirements of the work to the contractor. Illustrated by the plans. Together, the plans and specifications form the construction documents of the bid package or contract.

State Register of Historic Places Similar to the National Register, cataloguing historic sites within a given state. Administered by the State Historic Preservation Office. Applications can usually be made to the State and National Registers simultaneously.

Subcontractor A person or firm who has a direct contract with a prime contractor to perform a portion of the contractor's work.

Substantial Completion Point in a construction project when the work is basically finished, although clean up or details may require further attention.

Surety A company that secures a contracting firm with a bond, promising to pay its debts in case of default.

Unit Price Contract A contract in which payment is defined for a unit (for example, a window, or a square foot of roofing) and the total cost is based on the number of units installed/completed.

Warranty A legally enforceable assurance of the quality or duration of a product (as in a manufacturer's warranty) or of work performed (as in a contractor's warranty).

Workers' Compensation Insurance Insurance covering liability of an employer to employees for injury, sickness, disease, or death arising from the job.

Zoning Code Local government regulation concerning use of land and buildings.

Resources

New York Landmarks Conservancy

The New York Landmarks Conservancy's Sacred Sites Program is the only statewide initiative of its kind, offering congregations of all denominations financial and technical assistance to maintain and restore their historic buildings. Each year, hundreds of thousands of dollars in matching grants are awarded to support planning and restoration projects. In addition, the Conservancy publishes hands-on technical guides, organizes workshops for building caretakers, and publishes Common Bond, *an easy-to-understand journal on the preservation of religious structures.*

141 Fifth Avenue
New York, NY 10010
800-880-NYLC or
212-995-5260
www.nylandmarks.org

Preservation League of New York State

Offers grant programs (especially for nonprofits in rural or upstate New York), legal and technical assistance, and an advocacy network.

44 Central Avenue
Albany, NY 12206
518-462-5658
www.preservenys.org

New York State Office of Parks, Recreation and Historic Preservation - Bureau of Historic Sites

Links New Yorkers to the State and National Registers of Historic Places. Information about designation and research assistance are provided by field representatives according to county.

Peebles Island
P.O. Box 219
Waterford, NY 12188
518-237-8643
http://nysparks.state.ny.us/

▶ Preservation organizations throughout the United States

Partners for Sacred Places

Provides contacts and resources from around the country for maintaining and developing houses of worship. Keeps track of organizations similar to those in New York (listed above) in other states and regions.

1700 Sansom Street, Tenth Floor

Philadelphia, PA 19103

215-567-3234

www.sacredplaces.org

National Conference of State Historic Preservation Officers

Maintains contact information for the State Historic Preservation Offices in US states and territories.

444 North Capitol Street NW, Suite 342

Washington, DC 20001

202-624-5465

http://www.sso.org/ncshpo/shpolist.htm

National Alliance of Statewide Preservation Organizations

Has catalogued major preservation groups in most states.

c/o Preservation Alliance of Virginia

700 Harris Street, Suite 203

Charlottesville, VA 22903

804-984-4484

www.vapreservation.org/link-2.html#other-groups

National Trust for Historic Preservation

Provides general preservation information and offers a wide variety of publications.

National Office

1785 Massachusetts Avenue NW

Washington, DC 20036

202-588-6000

www.nthp.org

www.preservationbooks.org

Interfaith Coalition on Energy

Provides energy-saving advice nationally through publications and workshops (direct consultation is available in the greater Philadelphia area).

7217 Oak Avenue

Melrose Park, PA 19027

215-635-1122

The American Institute of Architects

Provides listings of member architects throughout the country; its Web site also has a guide to selecting and working with an architect.

1735 New York Avenue NW

Washington, DC 20006

800-AIA-3837

www.aia.org/consumer/

▶ Recommended preservation guides

Secretary of the Interior's Standards for the Treatment of Historic Properties

The US government's recommendations concerning historic properties contains clear, basic information on the values of preservation.

National Parks Service

P.O. Box 37127

Washington, DC 20013

202-343-9578

www2.cr.nps.gov/tps/secstan1.htm

Preservation Briefs

The Secretary of the Interior's preservation briefs contain practical statistics, useful history, and applicable repair techniques for a wide variety of building elements. Published by Heritage Preservation Services of the National Parks Service.

P.O. Box 37127

Washington, DC 20013

202-343-9578

www2.cr.nps.gov/tps/briefs/presbhom.htm

▶ Preservation and conservation Web sites

The American Institute for Conservation of Historic and Artistic Works has basic information about building conservators and useful guidelines for hiring one.
http://aic.Stanford.edu/

The International Council on Monuments and Sites is a professional association that reports on worldwide preservation. www.icomos.org

The National Parks Service offers basic advice on envisioning and planning a preservation project.
http://www2.cr.nps.gov/tps/care/goodguides.htm

Preserve & Protect is a nonprofit that hosts historic preservation and environmental protection Web sites, with good connections to New York organizations. www.preserve.org

PreservationDirectory.com collects resources and research tools for historic preservation and cultural resource management.

Save America's Treasures hosts links to national preservation programs and funding vehicles.
www.saveamericastreasures.org/resources.htm

▶ Periodicals of interest

Comfort & Light
Published by the Interfaith Coalition on Energy
7217 Oak Avenue
Melrose Park, PA 19027
215-635-1122

Common Bond
Published by the New York Landmarks Conservancy. Articles are available online.
141 Fifth Avenue
New York, NY 10010
800-880-NYLC or
212-995-5260
www.nylandmarks.org/publications/commonbond.html

E & A (Environment & Art)
Published by Liturgy Training Publications
1800 North Hermitage Avenue
Chicago, IL 60622-1101
800-993-4213

Faith and Form
Published by the Interfaith Forum on Religion, Art, and Architecture
3220 N Street NW
Washington, DC 20007-2829
http://members.tripod.com/faithNform/

Old House Journal
One Thomas Circle NW Suite 600
Washington, DC 20005
202-234-3797
www.oldhousejournal.com

Preservation
Published by the National Trust for Historic Preservation
1785 Massachusetts Avenue NW
Washington, DC 20036
www.nationaltrust.org/magazine/

Traditional Building
Published by Historical Trends Corporation
69A Seventh Avenue
Brooklyn, NY 11217
718-636-0788
www.traditional-building.com

▶ For product information

A few home improvement Web sites contain links to suppliers and products. Many companies will send free literature about their products, which may be helpful for developing a scope of work.

Old House Journal maintains a Web site that complements its magazine. It contains a chat room, links to products, and links to the National Parks Service's Preservation Briefs.
www.oldhousejournal.com

The Web site of This Old House provides advice and information about the products and techniques featured on its public television program.
http://www.pbs.org/wgbh/thisoldhouse/

Like its published counterpart, Traditional Building's Web site contains information about many products and suppliers.
www.traditional-building.com

▶ Fundraising

The Complete Guide to Capital Campaigns for Historic Churches and Synagogues **by** Peggy Powell Dean and Susanna A. Jones.
A comprehensive guide to managing fundraising campaigns, available from Partners for Sacred Places (contact information listed above).

The Foundation Center
79 Fifth Avenue
New York, New York 10003
212-620-4230
www.fdncenter.org
Provides searchable access to thousands of grant-makers and foundations throughout the United States, in addition to basic information on researching and applying for grants. Web site has further information and locations outside of New York.

Private foundations may also be researched through Grantsmart at www.grantsmart.org.

There are many, many links to sites related to fundraising through Princeton University, at www.princeton.edu/One/research/netlinks.html.

Order form

The Landmarks Conservancy *has several publications for caretakers of older houses of worship. Practical, thorough, and easy to understand, they speak to the issues confronted by congregations everyday.*

Inspecting and Maintaining Religious Properties
A workbook with text, photographs, and drawings demonstrating how to evaluate the building envelope and structural system of a house of worship; also describes how to reduce energy costs and approach ongoing maintenance.

Managing Repair & Restoration Projects: A Congregation's How-to Guide
The only book of its kind: a step-by-step explanation of effective planning and management for building projects of all sizes.

Common Bond
A seasonal journal covering both the technical and the administrative aspects of caring for older houses of worship, written for laypeople and clergy but also read by design professionals and contractors.

For credit card orders,
fax to 212-995-5268; attention: Publications.
Or call 212-995-5260 with your request.

Purchases by check may be mailed to:
Publications
New York Landmarks Conservancy
141 Fifth Avenue
New York, New York 10010

The New York Landmarks Conservancy is a nonprofit organization that preserves architecturally, historically, and culturally significant buildings by providing financial and technical assistance to their owners.

Title	Quantity	Amount
Managing Repair & Restoration Projects: A Congregation's How-to Guide	_____	$_____

Per book: $20.00 + $1.65 NY State sales tax* + $3.50 shipping

Inspecting and Maintaining Religious Properties	_____	$_____

Per book: $15.00 + $1.24 NY State sales tax* + $3.50 shipping

Common Bond, the jounal of the Conservancy's Sacred Sites Program	_____	$_____

Contributions above $15 *(per subscription)* support the Sacred Sites Program
Recommended giving levels
$15 Subscriber / $25 Friend / $50 Associate / $100 Advocate

Total cost $_____

Name

Institution

Shipping address

Credit card   ○ Visa   ○ Mastercard   ○ American Express
Number

Expiration date   Billing zip code

Signature

○   Check here if this is a mail order with check enclosed.
Please make checks payable to the New York Landmarks Conservancy.

*NY State sales tax is not applicable to out-of-state buyers or tax-exempt institutions.